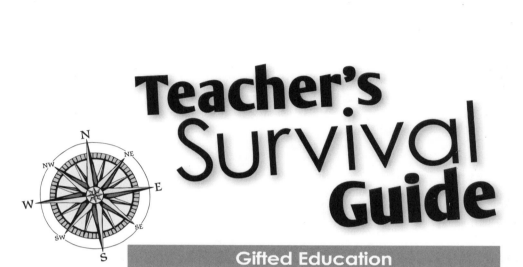

Teacher's Survival Guide

Gifted Education

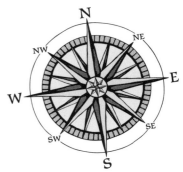

Teacher's Survival Guide

Gifted Education

Julia L. Roberts, Ed.D., and Julia Roberts Boggess

PRUFROCK PRESS INC.

WACO, TEXAS

Dedication

This book is the first one that we have written as a mother-daughter team, and we would like to dedicate it to Elizabeth, Caroline, Jane Ann, and Claire—Julia's four grand-girls and Julie's daughter, Claire, and nieces.

In addition, we would like to dedicate this book to all of the children and young people with whom we have worked over the years in classes as well as in summer and Saturday programs.

Library of Congress Cataloging-in-Publication Data

Roberts, Julia L. (Julia Link)
Teacher's survival guide : gifted education / by Julia Link Roberts and Julie Roberts Boggess.
   p. cm.
Includes bibliographical references.
ISBN 978-1-59363-538-1 (pbk.)
1. Gifted children--Education. 2. Teachers of gifted children. I. Boggess, Julie Roberts, 1972- II. Title.

LC3993.R6125 2011
371.95--dc22

2011010725

Edited by Lacy Compton

Layout Design by Raquel Trevino

ISBN-13: 978-1-59363-538-1

Printed in the United States of America.

At the time of this book's publication, all facts and figures cited are the most current available. All telephone numbers, addresses, and website URLs are accurate and active. All publications, organizations, websites, and other resources exist as described in the book, and all have been verified. The authors and Prufrock Press Inc. make no warranty or guarantee concerning the information and materials given out by organizations or content found at websites, and we are not responsible for any changes that occur after this book's publication. If you find an error, please contact Prufrock Press Inc.

Prufrock Press Inc.
P.O. Box 8813
Waco, TX 76714-8813
Phone: (800) 998-2208
Fax: (800) 240-0333
http://www.prufrock.com

Table of Contents

Acknowledgments

So many people have offered ideas to be included in this book. We are especially appreciative of our colleagues across the country who have written pieces that highlight their areas of expertise and interests.

Writers always need readers for their manuscripts. We appreciate the willingness and dedication of our readers, Tracy Inman and Carolyn Hagaman.

We are also grateful to Gail Hiles for the careful, professional work on the tables and figures included in this book.

Introduction

Teacher's Survival Guide: Gifted Education was written as a starting point for teachers who are new to gifted education, whether they are new to teaching or not. As a survival guide for your first years in gifted education, this resource should be a collection of information, advice, and suggestions you turn to again and again.

Teacher's Survival Guide: Gifted Education is just that—a survival kit filled with basic information on gifted education and strategies for helping gifted kids soar. The goal is to help you recognize and address the needs of gifted children, encourage their creativity, and apply strategies to remove the learning ceiling. It is written for educators interested in learning about gifted children and young people, both those who want to brush up on what is current in the field as well as those who are new to gifted education. The information also can be shared with parents, as the book is a very basic, easy-to-read resource for introducing gifted education. After all, it was written as a "survival guide."

The chapters in this book are short and to the point, even though each could be the topic for a longer work. They are written this way to bring you key information and resources on the many topics pertinent to teachers of gifted and advanced learners. The resources in each chapter's Survival Toolkit will guide you as you begin in gifted education, with the goal that you will thrive, not just survive, with their help. Several chapters will have short pieces called Survival Secrets, written by experts in the field of gifted education who share their experiences and provide advice that will help you understand specific topics in gifted education. Chapters also include leading questions to guide your thinking, tips to highlight important points, and quotations that you may want to remember.

As a mother-daughter team, we truly have enjoyed writing this book. Julie is a librarian at Pearre Creek Elementary School in Williamson County, TN. She has had experience as a gifted resource teacher and as a kindergarten and first-grade teacher. She has taught many sessions of summer and Saturday programs for young people who are gifted and talented in grades 1–8. Julia is a teacher educator who has prepared hundreds of gifted resource teachers and other educators in gifted education in the course of their graduate study. As the founding and current Executive Director of The Center for Gifted Studies at Western Kentucky University, she has directed 28 summers of programming for hundreds of gifted children.

We hope that you will learn much from *Teacher's Survival Guide: Gifted Education* and share the important information you learn with your colleagues and your students' parents.

Happy reading. Welcome to the world of gifted education.

Julia Link Roberts and Julia Roberts Boggess

1 Let's Start at the Very Beginning: Who Are Gifted Children?

Gifted children are perishable.—Troy Coleman, parent

Key Question
- What definitions for gifted children do your school, school district, and state use?

What Does "Gifted and Talented" Mean?

Let's start the conversation by looking at children who are gifted and talented. Who are they? What terminology is used in the United States in reference to these young people? What are gifted children called in your school, district, and state? What categories of giftedness are recognized where you teach?

Children and young people who are gifted and talented constitute a group that is quite diverse. They come from all ethnic and racial backgrounds, all socio-economic levels, and all geographic locations. They may speak any language, and they may have a disability, yet have advanced abilities. Gifted children represent a variety of interests and areas of talent. Even within the category of giftedness, there is a wide range of abilities and talents. The level of achievement and talent development often depends upon opportunities available. Many gifted individuals learn to underachieve early in their educational experience, but that does not have to be the case. Others have opportunities that allow them to thrive in school. Indeed, "diverse" is the descriptor that best characterizes children who are gifted and talented as well as the experiences and interests they bring to classrooms.

Perhaps the type of giftedness that most people understand best is athletic giftedness. Recently, headlines in a local paper used the term *gifted* to describe both an outstanding quarterback and a highly sought-after basketball recruit. The public admires those who are gifted in these athletic abilities, whether the talent is demonstrated in basketball, football, tennis, baseball, or golf. Some young people have natural athletic abilities, and consequently, they get coaching to develop their abilities. If every young person had the same intensity of coaching, would they all qualify for the varsity team? Of course not. They would not all develop into outstanding athletes, yet all children deserve the opportunity to try—to see if they will develop their skills and abilities to a high level. Those who demonstrate exceptional athletic abilities should not be held back because the other children around them do not perform at the same high level, just as those who are academically gifted should not be held back or made to do the same low-level work as their peers. The public seems to understand that not all people are gifted at running, throwing, or shooting baskets, yet they expect someone labeled as academically gifted to be gifted in all areas. However, an outstanding basketball player will not shine equally in every sport. Much like gifted athletes, gifted children usually do not display the same level of ability and interest in everything they do.

Several states include children who are gifted and talented as one category of exceptional or special education. The main difference between gifted children and other exceptional children is that a gifted child is identified by his strength or strengths rather than by a deficiency. Strengths do not make children look needy (they don't create sympathy for children who are gifted and talented), yet strengths create needs just as deficiencies do. Gifted children are just as different from the average learner as are children who are exceptional due to a disability. For example, a gifted child may be able to learn information quickly and at complex levels while a child with a learning disability may need more time to learn and a basic presentation of the materials to make adequate progress. Or a gifted child may be advanced in one or more content areas while another child of the same age may need to begin at a different level. All exceptional children, including gifted children, require special accommodations in order for each one to make continuous progress. Of course, ongoing learning is the purpose of going to school.

Definitions of Giftedness

The specific word used to refer to gifted children differs by state and individual. The National Science Board (2010) "alternately refers to the children and young people who have the most potential to become STEM innovators as 'talented and motivated' or 'high-ability' or 'gifted'" (p. 6). Some states choose to call these children *advanced learners* or *gifted and talented*. Still another term used to refer to gifted children is *highly capable learners*. Some people think it is important to put the children first, as in *children who are gifted and talented* and *children with gifts and talents*. The most important point to remember is to know the terminology used to refer to children who are gifted and talented in your district and state.

States also differ in the categories of giftedness that they recognize. Some states use intellectual giftedness only, while other states name several categories of giftedness. Six categories were included in the Marland Report (1972): general intellectual ability, a specific academic area, creative or productive thinking, leadership, the visual and performing arts, and psychomotor abilities. Soon after the Marland Report was issued, psychomotor ability was eliminated as one of those categories. Psychomotor giftedness continues to be important, but, as mentioned earlier, schools and the public already support athletic talent development, so gifted education funding could not also be used to support sports programs (psychomotor ability). A child can be identified as gifted in one or more of the five remaining categories.

The Jacob K. Javits Gifted and Talented Students Education Act (1988) defined gifted children as:

> Children and youth with outstanding talent perform or show the potential for performing at remarkably high levels of accomplishment when compared with others of their age, experience, or environment.
>
> These children and youth exhibit high performance capability in intellectual, creative, and/or artistic areas, possess an unusual leadership capacity, or excel in specific academic fields. They require services or activities not ordinarily provided by the schools.
>
> Outstanding talents are present in children and youth from all cultural groups, across all economic strata, and in all areas of human endeavor. (Cited in U.S. Department of Education, 1993, p. 3)

The federal definition of giftedness is as follows:

> (22) GIFTED AND TALENTED.—The term "gifted and talented", when used with respect to students, children, or youth, means students, children, or youth who give evidence of high achievement capability in areas

such as intellectual, creative, artistic, or leadership capacity, or in specific academic fields, and who need services or activities not ordinarily provided by the school in order to fully develop those capabilities. (No Child Left Behind Act, P.L. 107-110 [Title IX, Part A, Definition 22]; 2002)

The National Association for Gifted Children (NAGC; 2010b) issued a position paper on terminology in gifted education (see http://www.nagc.org for a copy) that defined giftedness as follows:

Gifted individuals are those who demonstrate outstanding levels of aptitude (defined as an exceptional ability to reason and learn) or competence (documented performance or achievement in top 10% or rarer) in one or more domains. Domains include any structured area of activity with its own symbol system (e.g., mathematics, music, language) and/or set of sensorimotor skills (e.g., painting, dance, sports). (p. 1)

Conclusion

Find the definition of gifted children used by your school, school district, and state, and clarify its meaning. Make it your responsibility to find out what will guide the identification of gifted children where you live. Are they called "advanced learners" or "children with gifts and talents"? The name is only the starting point, but what you do to recognize their needs and develop their potentials makes a lifelong difference.

Various labels for gifted children will be used in this book. The next chapter discusses the responsibilities of teachers of gifted students.

Survival Tips

O A gifted child's area of greatest strength is also his area of greatest need. Remember that a gifted child's needs are just as intense and different from the average child's, as are the needs of any other exceptional or special learners.

O Parents and teachers both need to know the definition of giftedness used in their school and district.

Survival Toolkit

- *The NAGC Mile Marker Series: Your Road Map for Supporting Gifted Children* (http://www.nagc.org/NAGCMileMarker.aspx): This resource is a CD-ROM that will do just what the title says—start you on your journey in supporting gifted education. It is divided into five sections, or mile markers. This resource provides a lot of information to get started in gifted education.

2 Find Out What You Do First

A good program for the gifted increases their involvement and interest in learning through the reduction of the irrelevant and the redundant.—Sidney P. Marland, Jr.

Key Question

- What are the laws and regulations for gifted education in your school, district, and state?

Getting Started as a Gifted Teacher: Asking Questions

Getting a job offer or a new teaching assignment is both exciting and daunting. You may be starting as a gifted resource teacher. You may be assigned to a single classroom, multiple classrooms, an entire school, or a pull-out room. It is also possible that you are a classroom teacher with a new interest in addressing the needs of gifted students in your classroom or your school has a new focus on ensuring that all children, including those who are gifted and talented, make continuous progress. Whether you are a veteran teacher or new to teaching, you are about to embark on an exciting new role—one that involves teaching advanced young learners. This survival guide is written with the goal of helping you launch yourself into this new role in a highly successful style.

You have likely taken graduate courses in gifted education, or perhaps you are starting your graduate classes now. It is even possible that your state does not require teachers to take gifted classes before teaching in a gifted program, so your education will come via workshops or classes you take because you want to learn more about teaching children who are gifted and talented. No matter your preparation, your most pressing questions are likely "Where do I start?" and "What do I do first?"

Your starting place may be to do some homework on what is mandated or expected for gifted education in your school, district, and state. The website of your state department of education will be a profitable place to start looking to see what is required in the way of services for children who are gifted and talented. The National Association for Gifted Children's website (http://www.nagc. org/index.aspx?id=609&gbs) has links to all of the state associations for gifted children to assist you in finding out more information. Does your state have laws that include children who are gifted and talented and list requirements for their education? Does your state have a regulation for gifted education? Does your school board have a policy on gifted education? Does your school district have a handbook of policies and procedures for gifted education? If the answer to any of these questions is yes, then you need to have copies of the laws, policies, and procedures to guide you as you prepare for your new responsibilities.

Roles and Responsibilities

Another early question to ask is what your responsibilities will be. There are many variations in programs and services for children and young people who are gifted and talented. Which ones characterize your new situation? Does your state refer to services offered to gifted children or to programs for them? It is important to define your role, as you can't be everything to everyone.

The role of a gifted resource teacher has many variations. You may have an entire class of students who are gifted and talented. You may be the resource teacher who is responsible for delivering services within a school. More challenging, you may be the educator responsible for delivering services for gifted children within an entire school district or in more than one school within the district. Yet another possibility is that you will be a teacher in a magnet program for gifted children, which could incorporate a one-day-a-week service model, allowing you only one day each week to teach your students.

You must learn what responsibilities you will have in your new position. Asking questions will be your way to begin defining your responsibilities. For example, you will need to ask who your supervisor is because you will need to ask a lot of questions of that individual. What expectations does your supervisor have for you? Who is responsible for establishing your schedule, and who can suggest input about that schedule? Talk with the person who had your position previously in order to see the "lay of the land." Also talk with your supervisor (who may be a district gifted coordinator or a building principal) to make sure that you fully understand all of his or her expectations for you in your new position.

Perhaps you do not have a new position, but rather a new emphasis in your school or in your Professional Learning Community (PLC) on being certain that gifted kids are stretched in terms of what they are capable of learning. What is your plan for ensuring that you know how to challenge all children in the classroom? What strategies will allow you to differentiate instruction in order to address the wide range of learning needs? Even if you have an entire class of young people who are all gifted and talented, remember that gifted children represent diverse needs and have a range of abilities and interests.

Most of all, you need to be ready to start your new position. To do that you must be clear on which categories of giftedness are recognized in your school, district, and state. In some states, the category of gifted just includes intellectually gifted children. In a few states, there are five categories of giftedness—intellectual giftedness as well as giftedness in a specific academic area, creativity, leadership, and the visual and performing arts. In those cases, the programs or services must match the category of giftedness. Remember, gifted children don't appear to have learning needs on the surface, as their areas of strength create their needs. The gifted teacher's role is to support gifted children academically as well as socially and emotionally. That support certainly includes providing opportunities for each student to make continuous progress in his areas of strength or giftedness.

Understanding Programs and Services

It is very important to understand and use appropriate terminology when communicating with gifted children and their educators and parents. Do you talk about a gifted program or gifted services for children in your school? The terms *gifted program* and *gifted services* are not synonymous, although you may find they are used interchangeably.

Gifted program tends to communicate that there is one service for gifted children. The downside of calling your service "the gifted program" is that it implies that children are either gifted or not. The other possibility is to give the program a specific name, such as Project Challenge or SOAR, so it is one of several services, including such options as acceleration in math or reading and differentiation in the classroom.

Speaking about services rather than the gifted program allows you to share the responsibility for addressing the needs (remember—needs stem from their strengths) of gifted children. You want all staff members to feel responsible for ensuring that all children, including those who are gifted and talented, make continuous progress. Services are offered by various educators and not just by the gifted resource teacher or teachers.

Terminology makes a difference in your message, so check out what terms describe gifted education practices in your school, district, and state. You should also know the key resources for basic information about gifted education, including:

- your state's gifted regulations,
- state laws that impact the education of gifted young people,
- your school district's school board policy on gifted education, and
- your school district's handbook for gifted education.

Knowing the Standards

The NAGC Pre-K–Grade 12 Gifted Programming Standards: A Blueprint for Quality Gifted Education (2010a) is a useful reference that will guide you, as well as educators in your school and district, as you develop services for children who are gifted and talented. Being familiar with the standards will provide confidence in your practices and will assist you as you assess progress in reaching those standards. You will find the standards on the National Association for Gifted Children website (http://www.nagc.org/index.aspx?id=546).

Conclusion

Getting started in your new position or with your new interest in gifted education is admirable. Locate important information from your school, district, and state to ensure that you make a positive start. Find the people who can help you know the laws and regulations, as well as the terminology, for you to incorporate in ways that will be beneficial for the children you are teaching. It always pays off to educate yourself before you launch into a new area of education.

Survival Tips

- Launch yourself into gifted education by first finding out the "lay of the land" in your school, district, and state.

- Make sure parents know what your school, district, and state have as regulations and laws that set what services will be offered or could be available for young people who are gifted and talented.

Survival Toolkit

- *The Davidson Institute for Talent Development* (http://www. davidsongifted.org): This site is another ready source of current information on gifted education in all states.

- *National Association for Gifted Children* (http://www.nagc.org): This website is a source of information about what is going on in gifted education in all states.

- *State of the States* (http://www.nagc.org/index.aspx?id=1051): The Council of State Directors of Programs for the Gifted and the National Association for Gifted Children publish *State of the States,* a report issued every 2 years. This report tells you a lot about what your state does or does not do for children who are gifted and talented. The *State of the States* provides an overview of definition, policy, and funding for gifted education in your state.

3 Building Broad-Based Support for Gifted Education

There is nothing so unequal as the equal treatment of unequal people.—Thomas Jefferson

---

Key Questions

- What is your message as you speak out on behalf of children who are gifted and talented?
- With whom should you be prepared to advocate for gifted education?

Why Advocate for Gifted Children?

To advocate means to speak out on behalf of someone or something. Speaking out in support of gifted education is incredibly important. Here are a few reasons why gifted children need advocates and support for appropriate educational opportunities:

1. Gifted children will provide a disproportionate number of leaders for our future. Those are leaders that your community, state, and country need.

2. Myths about gifted children are so widely believed that advocates are needed to provide accurate information. Debunking myths about gifted children is important in order for educators and parents to understand the needs of gifted young people—a prerequisite for challenging them at appropriate levels.

3. Children who are not challenged actually may lose ground in school, both in terms of brain development (more dendrites result from novelty) and achievement (every child should make at least a year's achievement gain for each year spent in school). Much to the surprise of many people, advanced students often do not make a year's achievement gain in a year as they frequently are not challenged in school.

4. Quality educational opportunities for all children (all children includes advanced learners) constitute an economic development strategy. Businesses and industries that depend upon and value innovation will want to locate the places where quality educational opportunities are provided. The advantage is both for the children and their future employers.

5. The purpose of school is for children to learn on an ongoing basis. It is the school's responsibility to ensure that all children make continuous progress, including those who are gifted and talented.

6. Your future and our country's future depend upon the children who are currently in school. What an important reason that is to support gifted education!

Just think about the small children you know and consider factors that will determine their futures. At the moment, their futures are bright. What needs to happen to ensure both their futures and your own?

One expert in gifted education, Lynette Baldwin, highlights the responsibility of and opportunities for teachers to become advocates. She encourages all educators to advocate for children with special needs, including those who are gifted and talented.

◇◇

SURVIVAL SECRETS FOR GIFTED TEACHERS

Lynette Baldwin

The job description for a teacher of gifted and talented children is expected to include identifying gifted students, providing a variety of differentiated services to meet the students' needs, and doing the myriad volumes of paperwork that gather in piles on the desk. The missing piece of the job description, and the piece that may cause great surprise to the educator, is that the role of advocate must be assumed. Going into the job, many new teachers of gifted and talented children *assume* that colleagues and parents are as eager as they are to see that gifted children are challenged. It's wonderful when the support is there. It can be disheartening when it's missing. That's when the role of the advocate must kick in.

What does one do to become an advocate?

- First of all, believe in the importance of meeting the needs of gifted children. Develop the passion.
- You are the resident expert. Know your stuff. Know the laws and regulations. Know the research on gifted and talented children—their nature and needs as well as appropriate educational opportunities. Know the myths and the truths about gifted students. Know the individual students.
- From the information and knowledge of your audience(s), craft a clear message and state it often.
- Find supporters of gifted education and nurture them. Educate those who are not supporters in a positive way. There are many ways to do this—some overt, some . . . maybe not! At the same time, you are developing positive relationships among colleagues, parents, and members of the community, and those relationships go far toward strengthening acceptance of giftedness and the need for GT services.
- Be persistent. Rome wasn't built in a day, and neither will be support for gifted and talented services. However, over time, the number of supporters will increase and changes for the better will be made.

Being a teacher advocate for gifted students is just as important as the other aspects of the job description for educators of gifted children. You believe in what you're doing and want others to believe in appropriate opportunities for gifted and talented children as well. This passion will give you courage. Go forth, teacher-advocator! Make a difference!

Lynette Baldwin
Executive Director, Kentucky Association for Gifted Education
Paducah, KY

Who Should Advocate for Gifted Children and How Do They Do So?

Parents, educators, and citizens need to advocate for appropriate educational opportunities for gifted young people, and you, as a teacher of gifted children, need to have a strong, accurate voice. As a teacher of gifted children, you have many ways to be an advocate. One of those ways is to be a member of decision-making groups like school councils so that you can be a voice representing young people who are gifted and talented. You also can advocate in organizations in which you are active. You can present sessions at conferences that educate your fellow teachers on the needs of gifted young people and strategies to address their needs. Joining your state's gifted organization is a great way to learn about opportunities and new developments, so that you are current about best practices in gifted education. You can also be an important influence with parents, informing them of their child's rights and learning needs. Overall, the best way to advocate is to look for ways that you can help fellow educators and parents better understand the unique and diverse needs of children who are gifted and talented.

Advocacy involves educating others on an issue or a cause in addition to speaking out on that issue. Teachers must be educated so that they can appropriately speak out on behalf of the needs of gifted children. Sometimes that may mean correcting the myths about gifted children that are spoken so freely because they are believed so readily. Sometimes that may mean going to a seminar on the social-emotional needs of gifted children. Sometimes it is speaking up at a meeting to ask the questions highlighted in *Mind the (Other) Gap* (Plucker, Burroughs, & Song, 2010). The report noted two questions that should be posed whenever educational decisions are made (by legislators, educators in the central office or at the school level, and parents).

1. How will this [decision] affect our brightest students?
2. How will this [decision] help other students begin to achieve at high levels?

What Parents Must Know

Parents must know the guidelines and rights for the education of gifted children. An essential question to ask is: Are children making continuous progress? If the answer is no, then policies and practices to ensure continuous progress should become the focus of advocacy efforts.

Policies put best practices in place without the need to fight the battle each year. The following are examples of useful policies for keeping children learning on an ongoing basis. Check out other examples in Chapter 19, which includes the Gold Standard School checklist.

1. Cut-off points for starting school (a few children are ready sooner than others).
2. Requirements for graduation from high school—for example, the requirement to have a math class each year in high school differs from requiring four math credits (one requirement hampers early graduation while the other doesn't).
3. Performance-based credit—Such a policy makes it possible to demonstrate what one knows and is able to do to meet established standards for a course and opt out of that particular class or requirement.

Support Gifted Education at All Levels by Joining Advocacy Groups

Most states have a state organization with a focus on advocating for gifted education. Your state gifted education organization will have guidance for you in terms of setting up a local affiliate group. Groups can be specifically for parents or for educators, but they seem to be more effective when parents and educators work together to understand and advocate for children who are gifted and talented. NAGC has an advocacy packet that can be useful in getting started as an organization (see http://www.nagc.org). Remember that it is good practice to look around for materials that have already been developed. These ready-made materials will save time and allow you to take advantage of available expertise. Of course, you must give appropriate credit to those who have developed the materials you choose to use.

There are also national and international organizations that focus on advocacy for children who are gifted and talented. They offer resources as well as professional development opportunities to learn more about strategies for addressing the needs of gifted children. Here is the contact information for some of the most active organizations that teachers can join:

The Association for the Gifted (TAG)
The Council for Exceptional Children
2900 Crystal Drive, Suite 1000
Arlington, VA 22202-3557
Telephone: (888) 232-7733
http://www.cectag.org

National Association for Gifted Children
1331 H Street NW, Suite 1001
Washington, DC 20005

Telephone: (202) 785-4268
nagc@nagc.org
http://www.nagc.org

Supporting Emotional Needs of the Gifted
P.O. Box 488
Poughquag, NY 12570
Telephone: (845) 797-5054
office@sengifted.org
http://www.sengifted.org

The World Council for Gifted and Talented Children (WCGTC)
Western Kentucky University
Gary A. Ransdell Hall
1906 College Heights Boulevard #11030
Bowling Green, KY 42101-1030
Telephone: (270) 745-4123
headquarters@world-gifted.org
https://www.world-gifted.org

Numbers count in advocacy. The Prichard Committee of Academic Excellence in Kentucky created the following example to highlight the importance of joining with others who share your interests (Roberts, 2006):

> If you think that you alone cannot do much to improve your school, you are probably right. You're more likely to get what you want for children if you work with others. If you collaborate with other parents and organizations, you can make a bigger difference than if you make requests on your own. There is strength and power in numbers.
>
> > 1 person = A fruitcake
> > 2 people = A fruitcake and a friend
> > 3 people = Troublemakers
> > 5 people = "Let's have a meeting"
> > 10 people = "We'd better listen"
> > 25 people = "Our dear friends"
> > 50 people = "A powerful organization"
>
> Although humorous, this description of the numbers required to move from a fruitcake to a powerful organization rings true. (p. 247)

Just as numbers count, so do relationships. You need to know the people who are in decision-making positions. That is not hard to do at the school level, but it is very important at the district level as well. Of course, decisions are also made at the state level, both by members of the legislature and by your state school board. Don't hesitate to provide them with information. After all, they represent you, and decisions they make will have a long-term impact on the children in your family as well as in your classroom, district, and state. It is easier to influence a decision before it is made than it is to change one after it is established in policy.

The important thing is for you to be well-informed about gifted children and their needs and willing to speak out on their behalf. It is also essential to help parents understand why their children must be learning at appropriately high levels. Parents must be informed so they can be advocates for excellence. After all, your future depends on doing just that.

Conclusion

The need exists for teachers of gifted and talented children to be advocates, making sure that students' learning needs are met both in and out of the classroom. Parents also should be encouraged to be advocates for their children, as should school and district administrators. One of the most important steps in advocacy is the sharing of your knowledge about gifted children with parents and fellow educators—remember that a little information can go a long way toward ensuring the development of our future leaders, thinkers, and innovators.

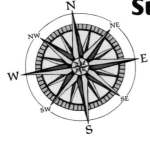

Survival Tips

- Knowing why you support gifted education will help you communicate those reasons to others.

- Make sure parents know why it is important to support gifted education.

- Be ready to ask two very important questions when decisions are being made: (1) How will this decision affect our brightest students?, and (2) How will this decision help other students begin to achieve at high levels? Most of the time, those questions could add to the discussion in positive ways for all children.

Survival Toolkit

- *Advocacy Toolkit* (http://www.nagc.org/index.aspx?id=36): This kit, designed for state and local advocates in gifted education, provides a variety of articles on advocacy, along with links to various NAGC resources, the Legislative Action Network, and a congressional directory so advocates can contact their U.S. Representatives and Senators.

- *Gifted Advocacy* (http://www.hoagiesgifted.org/advocacy.htm): This page on the Hoagies' Gifted Education Page website provides a wide variety of links to tips on advocating for gifted children.

- *Parenting for High Potential* (http://www.nagc.org/index.aspx?id=1180): This magazine is a great source of information on many topics, including advocacy. Julia Link Roberts and Tracy Ford Inman write a column on advocacy with practical suggestions on how to be an effective advocate and what you can advocate for in gifted education.

- *Starting and Sustaining a Parent Group to Support Gifted Children* (http://www.nagc.org/parentgroupeguide.aspx): This free guide from NAGC and Prufrock Press provides a multitude of tips and resources for parent advocates and for teachers wanting to help the parents of their students be more involved.

- *Using Public Relations Strategies to Advocate for Gifted Programming in Your School* (http://journals.prufrock.com/IJP/c.abs/gifted-child-today/volume28/issue1/article160): This article in *Gifted Child Today* is geared especially toward teachers who want to improve their advocacy efforts for gifted children.

- Lewis, J. (2008). *Advocacy for gifted children and gifted programs.* Waco, TX: Prufrock Press.

4 Don't Treat Gifted Children Like Wallpaper or Accessories

Nothing is more difficult than competing with a myth.—Lao Tsu

Key Question

- What is fact and what is fiction related to gifted children?

Sometimes people assume that gifted children will be okay, so they treat them like wallpaper: They take them for granted. Frankly, the people who assume that gifted children will make it on their own are mistaken. Gifted children and adolescents will not reach their potentials if educators and others make such faulty assumptions. The truth is that we all need for gifted children to reach their full potentials, as they will be represented in high numbers among our future leaders, innovators, and professionals.

Other times, educators and parents treat children who are gifted and talented as accessories. One example of treating gifted children as accessories is routinely using them as peer tutors in the classroom. Another example of treating these children as accessories is when they are valued for their test scores. Still another example is showcasing these children for something they can do that is precocious. It is shortsighted to value gifted students for peer tutoring, having high test scores, or performing at advanced levels. Instead, valuing a child for positive personal attributes, such as honesty and helpfulness, is very important, and doing so reinforces values in our communities and creates a promising future for these gifted children as well as for all children.

You need to know the facts so that you can counteract the myths. We'll discuss and debunk many of the myths about gifted children in the sections that follow.

Myth 1

Isn't proficiency an admirable goal for teachers to set for their students? Have you experienced being caught on the interstate in traffic that is so heavy that your progress comes to a halt? Compare the feeling you have when you are slowed down or even stopped in traffic with the feeling you have when you are moving right along in the flow of normal driving. That comparison will help you understand the frustration felt by advanced learners when they are "caught in the traffic" of a class that is focused on grade-level learning and bringing all children to proficiency. Remember, proficiency is an admirable goal unless you have already reached or exceeded that goal. Then proficiency is no goal at all, but a barrier to learning.

Myth 2

Aren't all children gifted? If the question refers to all children being special, then they certainly are. However, if "all children are gifted" refers to children performing at an advanced level in comparison to children their age, the answer is no. All fifth or eighth graders do not perform at the same level in mathematics, reading, or science any more than they are all able to shoot free throws, swim laps, or kick goals at exceptionally skilled levels. Some athletes are exceptional just as some children have exceptional abilities as writers, mathematicians, and scientists.

Myth 3

Don't gifted children come from middle- to high-income families? Gifted children come from all economic backgrounds, in both rural and urban areas. The challenge is that all gifted children need support to continue perform-ing at the highest levels. Children who are gifted and from low socioeconomic backgrounds need to know about opportunities, but also about where to find financial support to participate in opportunities. Otherwise, an opportunity gap develops and likely already exists. Likewise, gifted children come from a variety of cultural and ethnic backgrounds, speak a multitude of languages, and have a mixture of abilities.

Myth 4

Aren't children who are gifted and talented outstanding in all areas? Differences are evident among gifted children. A child may be advanced in reading, math, or any other subject, yet perform at grade level in another area. Or, the young person may be above grade level and ready for accelerated learning in several content areas. Still another child may be exceptional in creative thinking and need ongoing opportunities to use those creative thinking skills in various content areas. Further, some students who are gifted also have disabilities—for example, a gifted reader may have a handwriting disability that precludes him from doing well on written assignments. Remember, gifted children are diverse. They don't all have the same profiles of strengths or areas of giftedness.

Myth 5

Don't all gifted children make top grades? The answer is a resounding "no." All gifted children do not make outstanding grades; in fact, some of them are underachievers. The key to engaging all children in learning is to start where they are in their learning, rather than assuming that all fifth graders are at the same point and all need to learn the fifth-grade content. Preassessing students to determine what they know about a concept can make a world of difference in matching learning experiences to what the student knows and is able to do with the specific content being studied. (Chapter 11 provides a discussion of preassessment.) It is hard to stay motivated when you know most or all of the content. Remember the feeling you have when you are stuck in traffic? That's a feeling you don't want to repeat if you can avoid it.

Myth 6

Isn't it a good idea to use gifted children as peer tutors? The answer to that question may depend on how often a child is asked to peer tutor, if she enjoys peer tutoring, and whether she is effective as a peer tutor. The goal for each child is to learn on a continuing basis or to make continuous progress. Occasionally, it is fine for a child to peer tutor another; however, it is inappropriate for peer tutoring to interfere with a child's own learning. It is also important to keep in mind that a child who learns something so quickly and effortlessly will often not be effective as a teacher (another name for the tutor) working one-on-one with a student who is struggling to learn the content. Sometimes the peer tutoring is used to occupy the time of children who have mastered the assigned work. Instead, grouping for instructional purposes (see Chapter 13) can facilitate ongoing learning for children who have already mastered course objectives.

Myth 7

You don't need to worry about gifted kids because they will "get it" on their own. This myth is dangerous, as it leads to benign neglect as the assumption is made that it is okay to concentrate differentiation strategies on children who need to reach proficiency. Of course, those children are important, too; however, no children should be left out of opportunities to learn on an ongoing basis. Believing this myth leads to young people who underachieve and don't have the knowledge or skills to meet an academic challenge when they face one—which is bound to happen. These young people don't develop study skills because they have never needed them. What a loss!

Conclusion

Myths about gifted children and best practices for addressing their needs are prevalent and often believed to be factual. In fact, the mythology about gifted students is so widely believed that many outstanding educators are influenced by myths such as "Don't worry about gifted children, as they will 'get it' on their own." Teachers need to debunk these myths and work toward spreading accurate information about their gifted students.

Survival Tips

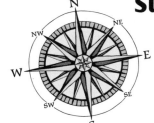

- Use your new expertise to correct myths that many experienced educators and the public in general believe to be true. Gifted children will benefit when you do.

- Parents also need to know what is myth and what is fact about gifted children. Share resources you have to help them be well informed about gifted education.

Survival Toolkit

- *Gifted Child Quarterly* (http://gcq.sagepub.com): The Fall 2009 issue of this journal was dedicated to the topic of demythologizing gifted education. It provides valuable information for learning what is and isn't true about gifted education.

- *Top 10 Myths in Gifted Education* (http://www.youtube.com/
  watch?v=MDJst-y_ptl): The Maryland Department of Education
  produced an effective video on myths about gifted children.
  This video can be educational for you and useful when sharing
  information to educate parents, fellow educators, and your students.

5 Recognizing Differences Among Gifted Children

Because talents manifest in numerous domains, children remain a very hetero-geneous group of people; as children, few to no claims would be equally true for the entire group of gifted students.—Tracy L. Cross (2011, p. 34)

Key Question

- What characteristics are typical of young people who are high achieving, gifted, and creative?

If you know characteristics that are typical of gifted and talented children, you will be prepared to recognize these students in your classroom. Remember, gifted children are a diverse group, so no set of characteristics will describe all of them.

One way to think about intellectually gifted children is that they learn at a faster pace and a more complex level than their age-peers. Think of the differences between high-speed and dial-up Internet connections. The processing time is quite different, and those different capabilities create very different expectations. The child who is intellectually gifted could be compared to high-speed Internet. This child who has experienced appropriately challenging learning experiences knows the joy of learning (just as you have enjoyed the speed of the Internet once you have switched from dial-up connections). People who have experienced both types of Internet connection—dial-up and high-speed—are quite impatient with the slower mode of connecting. Likewise, gifted children are likely not easy to engage in grade-level instruction if what they know and are able to do is beyond that level; in fact, for some gifted students, they are well beyond the level of instruction that is appropriate for most children their age. This comparison is offered to help you understand one difference in how children who are gifted and talented experience the world.

Gifted children have different abilities, talents, and interests, making them a very diverse group of individuals. What they share in common are advanced development and an intense interest in a particular content or talent area. Some children will show evidence of talent in numerous areas, but some will be advanced in one particular area. Gifted children won't look alike in your classroom either. You will miss many of them if you don't look for characteristics and behaviors that evidence themselves in many different ways.

Examples of Gifted Children

The following vignettes provide a few examples of children who are gifted and talented but have gifts and talents in different areas. As you read these, we hope you'll recognize that not all gifted children look alike.

James has had an insatiable curiosity since he was very young. He frequently takes things apart. He uses objects intended for one purpose for another because he sees that it will work to do so. Adults worry that something is "wrong" with him, as his constant questioning seems bothersome. The adults in his life need to realize that asking a good question is more important than having the right answer. A positive situation results when a teacher recognizes James's creative thinking abilities and provides opportunities for him to channel his thinking in productive ways.

Maria is very interested in sketching and spends time drawing as the teacher talks to the class. She is a willing learner, and she excels when her class projects allow her to incorporate her artistic abilities. If the teacher recognizes her interests and capitalizes on them, Maria will thrive in school. On the other hand, she is not likely to thrive if she is constantly reminded to put down her sketchbook and listen.

Ariana is advanced in all content areas—social studies, math, science, and language arts—and she is also quite accomplished at playing the violin. Sometimes she does not want to go to school and would prefer learning at home, where she can select the books and other resources to learn about topics at the level at which she is interested. She is happiest in school when she has various opportunities to make continuous progress.

Chad has been a leader among his age-peers since he entered school. He gets others to do whatever he asks, and usually his goals are good ones. Other young people are eager to hear what Chad has to say and usually follow his directions. Chad will benefit from services that develop his leadership skills. Without leadership training and chances to develop his skills, he will lose sight of positive ways to use his leadership capabilities.

Elizabeth is an outstanding reader, comprehending reading materials several levels above her current grade. She is especially interested in history and other social studies topics. In math, Elizabeth is at grade level. She thrives in school when she is clustered with other advanced readers who motivate each other as they discuss their advanced reading choices. She is unhappy when she is required to work on grade-level reading materials by a teacher who is afraid that she may have missed a reading skill or two.

The young people described above are gifted children, but advanced in different ways. In order for them to thrive in school, assignments must be differentiated in order to capitalize on what they do well and encourage their interests. Chapters 12 and 13 will describe strategies for differentiating assignments. A one-size-fits-all curriculum will not bring out the best in gifted children. Teachers must know their students' interests, needs, and abilities well in order for all of them to make continuous progress. The best way to address the needs of all types of gifted children is to remove the learning ceiling.

Comparing Characteristics of High Achievers, Gifted Learners, and Creative Thinkers

One way to look at the behaviors of children who are high achievers in comparison with those who are gifted learners is through a chart created by Kingore (2004) and shown in Table 1. The third column of this chart adds the behaviors of creative thinkers. This chart provides a good way to recognize differences among high-achieving, gifted, and creative children. The chart is a basic reference to use when helping colleagues understand that high-achieving students do not have the needs that gifted children do and how creative thinkers differ from other gifted children.

You may want to print off the Kingore chart and cut it into two strips—one for high-achieving students and one for gifted students. Then cut the characteristics into separate descriptors on individual strips and mix them up. The next step is to test your knowledge of the differences between high-achieving and

Table 1
High Achiever, Gifted Learner, Creative Thinker

A High Achiever . . .	A Gifted Learner . . .	A Creative Thinker . . .
Remembers the answers.	Poses unforeseen questions.	Sees exceptions.
Is interested.	Is curious.	Wonders.
Is attentive.	Is selectively mentally engaged	Daydreams; may seem off task.
Generates advanced ideas.	Generates complex, abstract ideas.	Overflows with ideas, many of which will never be developed.
Works hard to achieve.	Knows without working hard.	Plays with ideas and concepts
Answers the questions in detail.	Ponders with depth and multiple perspectives.	Injects new possibilities.
Performs at the top of the group.	Is beyond the group.	Is in own group.
Responds with interest and opinions.	Exhibits feelings and opinions from multiple perspectives.	Shares bizarre, sometimes conflicting opinions.
Learns with ease.	Already knows.	Questions: What if...
Needs 6 to 8 repetitions to master.	Needs 1 to 3 repetitions to master.	Questions the need for mastery.
Comprehends at a high level.	Comprehends in-depth, complex ideas.	Abstracts beyond original ideas.
Enjoys the company of age peers.	Prefers the company of intellectual peers.	Prefers the company of creative peers but often works alone.
Understands complex, abstract humor.	Creates complex, abstract humor.	Relishes wild, off-the-wall humor.
Grasps the meaning.	Infers and connects concepts.	Makes mental leaps: Aha!
Completes assignments on time.	Initiates projects and extensions of assignments.	Initiates more projects than will ever be completed.
Is receptive.	Is intense.	Is independent and unconventional.
Is accurate and complete.	Is original and continually developing.	Is original, ever changing, and misunderstood.
Enjoys school often.	Enjoys self-directed learning.	Enjoys creating.

Table 1, continued

A High Achiever . . .	A Gifted Learner . . .	A Creative Thinker . . .
Absorbs information.	Manipulates information.	Improvises.
Is a technician with expertise in a field.	Is an expert, abstracts beyond the field.	Is an inventor and idea generator.
Memorizes well.	Guesses and infers well.	Creates and brainstorms well.
Is highly alert and observant.	Anticipates and relates observations.	Is intuitive.
Is pleased with own learning.	Is self-critical.	Is never finished with possibilities.
Gets A's.	May not be motivated by grades.	May not be motivated by grades.
Is able.	Is intellectual.	Is idiosyncratic.

From *Differentiation: Simplified, Realistic, and Effective,* by B. Kingore, 2004, Figure 4.2, Austin, TX: Professional Associates Publishing. Copyright 2004 Professional Associates Publishing. Reprinted with permission.

gifted learners. If you can match these descriptors, then add the ones for children who are creative thinkers and test your ability to determine which descriptors are characteristic of each of the three types of learners on the Kingore chart.

Conclusion

Recognizing the strengths of all children is important, and it is necessary for educators to know the strengths of gifted children in particular. Remember, strengths are relative. For gifted children, their strengths are likely to manifest in achievement one or more grade levels above others in their class. Yet some gifted young people may perform several grades above their age-mates. The strengths of gifted children determine the areas in which they need advanced instruction if they are to make continuous progress. Matching learning experiences to the strengths that children have is the best way to ensure that they have the ongoing opportunity to learn at high levels. Continuous progress is the goal of schools, and differentiating instruction is the means to make continuous progress a reality for all children, including those who are gifted and talented.

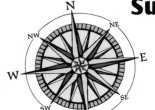

Survival Tips

- Learn to distinguish among the characteristics of children who are high achievers, gifted learners, and creative thinkers because their needs (based on their strengths) differ one from another.

- Parents also need to be familiar with characteristics of children who are gifted and creative thinkers. Parents often are the first to point out their children's learning needs to teachers and administrators, and they can provide insight into children's strengths and talents outside of school.

Survival Toolkit

- *Characteristics and Behaviors of the Gifted* (http://www.ri.net/gifted_talented/character.html): This site, sponsored by the Rhode Island State Advisory Committee on Gifted and Talented Education, contains an overview of the characteristics of gifted students, including information on their learning styles and creative abilities and highly gifted children.

- *Characteristics of Giftedness* (http://www.gifteddevelopment.com/What_is_Gifted/characgt.htm): Dr. Linda Silverman of the Gifted Development Center shares a list of the common characteristics of gifted children.

- *Definitions, Models, and Characteristics of Gifted Students* (http://www.prufrock.com/client/client_pages/Definitions_and_Characteristics/Definitions_and_Characteristics_of_Gifted_Students.cfm): This excerpt from *Identifying Gifted Students*, by Susan Johnsen, provides a thorough overview of how gifted children are identified.

- Kingore, B. (2001). *The Kingore Observation Inventory* (2nd ed.). Austin, TX: Professional Associates Publishing.

6 Identifying Gifted Students

Cast a wide net to identify all types of talents and to nurture potential in all demographics of students. To this end, we must develop and implement appropriate talent assessments at multiple grade levels and prepare educators to recognize potential, particularly among those individuals who have not been given adequate opportunities to transform their potential into academic achievement.
—National Science Board (2010, p. 3)

Key Question

- What are the regulations for identifying children who are gifted and talented in your school, district, and state?

Identification is a very important process, and one that must be taken seriously. Educators need to acknowledge that identification is not an exact science, so they must use best practices to guide the identification process. The purpose of identification is to provide assessment data to match the gifted services to the needs of the child. Teachers need to "zero in" on each student's readiness, interests, abilities, and talents. After all, educators must always be interested in ensuring that students have the most appropriate opportunities to learn at challenging levels, as well as to recognize and develop their talents. Data gathered during the identification process provide that important information.

. . . .

On an airplane trip, a woman across the aisle noticed what I was reading and asked if I was a teacher. After I responded yes, she followed up with questions and was eager to tell of two gifted children in her classroom the previous year. She remarked that she was so glad that they had gone on to a teacher who wasn't overwhelmed by the paperwork for recommending them to be assessed for the gifted program. She said that lots of teachers didn't want to bother with the paperwork. Of course, that may be the case for educators who don't see gifted children as having real needs. They miss the point that gifted children have needs emanating from their strengths rather than from deficiencies. A gifted child is every bit as needy as other exceptional learners if you examine how different they are from the average learner.

. . . .

Basic Points About Identification

There are a few basic points for you to remember when identifying children as gifted and talented:

1. *Identification must be defensible.* Educators need to know what procedures are to be followed and what assessments are to be used.

2. *Services must be matched to the area of identification.* That match is very important; in fact, it is the match that makes services defensible. For example, if the assessment is to identify young people who are exceptionally creative in their thinking, the services to be offered must acknowledge creative thinking ability and provide learning experiences to further develop their creative thinking capabilities.

3. *Diversity must be considered.* Procedures and assessments must be in place to provide appropriate assessments for children from diverse racial and ethnic backgrounds and from families with limited financial resources, as well as for those for whom English is not the first language and those who are twice-exceptional.

4. *The identification process must be ongoing, as talent emerges at different points in a school career.* It is never too late to recognize that a young person's ability is advanced when compared with her age-peers. Sometimes such abilities show up early, but not always.

5. *Services must provide continuous progress.* The purpose of identifying children in some area of giftedness and/or talent is to recognize the need for appropriate services to develop that area of talent or high interest. Continuous progress in an area of strength is necessary if talent is to develop or interest in an academic area is to flourish.

6. *Procedures must be followed.* Identification must follow the guidelines that the state and local school district have established. Educators can find out these guidelines by talking to gifted coordinators and school

administrators and by looking at their state department of education's website.

7. *Multiple measures must be used.* No single assessment should be used to determine giftedness, nor should one score exclude a child from being identified as gifted. These measures might include identification tests, rating scales (for teachers and parents to fill out), work samples, and portfolios.

8. *Use assessments to identify giftedness in diverse populations.* Assessments must be selected to maximize the opportunity for children who represent diverse populations to be identified as gifted in one or more categories of giftedness. For that reason, tests must not be culture-biased and nonverbal measures may need to be used to identify students.

9. *Offer professional development on identification.* If the school is under-identifying children from diverse backgrounds, professional development can be provided that will help teachers recognize giftedness and potential giftedness in these populations.

Type of Assessment for Various Categories of Giftedness

Different types of assessments are used to identify children as gifted in various categories. Assessments of aptitude may be administered to a group of students or to individual students, and they provide the means of identifying children as intellectually gifted. Assessments of achievement are used to identify children as gifted in a specific academic area. Measures of creative thinking are key to identifying children as gifted in creativity. Performances and portfolios provide evidence of giftedness in the visual and performing arts. Leadership is assessed through a portfolio and by using a sociogram to determine to whom children in the class look to solve problems and to lead in a project.

Defensible is the key word when it comes to identifying gifted children. Of course, the district or state's definition of giftedness will guide the selection of assessments for you to use as you gather data on children. Usually identification is a two-step process: first screening and then identification.

One expert on gifted education, Susan Johnsen, provides useful information about the identification process. She highlights information that is important to understand in order to implement defensible identification procedures.

◇◇

SURVIVAL SECRETS FOR IDENTIFYING GIFTED STUDENTS

Susan Johnsen

What do educators need to know about identifying gifted and talented students? Educators need to be aware of the characteristics of students with gifts and talents in order to identify them. They need to know that students may be gifted in one area and not another. For example, a student may be achieving above grade level in math, but on grade level in reading. Because other factors, such as cultural background, income level of the family, a disability, or even age, may also influence how students exhibit specific characteristics, educators need to understand how a student's characteristics interact with these factors and produce different behaviors. For example, a student who is twice-exceptional (i.e., is gifted and also identified as having a disability) may show critical thinking during science class, but not be able to read or write at grade level.

Next, educators need to create classroom environments that nurture talents and develop opportunities for students to accelerate and to think deeply about the content. Opportunities might include the use of long-term assignments, open-ended activities, contracting, independent research, compacting, preassessment, mentoring, above-grade-level materials, higher-level questions, and activities that emphasize depth or breadth in a specific subject area. Without an environment that is challenging and interesting, students with gifts and talents may not be recognized and may even hide what they already know. For example, it's not uncommon that kindergarten children will try to fit in and not show that they are able to read or do complex math problems. Educators should therefore be observant, focus on a child's strengths, and notice characteristics that might be indicative of high potential.

When selecting assessments for identification, educators need to align these with the characteristics of the students and with the services that they will receive. For example, if programming aims to develop students' abilities in mathematics, then the identification instruments would examine potential in that area. Assessments might include achievement tests in math, observations of students solving math problems, intelligence tests, teacher and parent checklists of characteristics demonstrating mathematical aptitude, and classroom projects involving math. Educators should notice that the assessments should include multiple sources of information (e.g., parents, students, teachers) and both quantitative and qualitative data. The assessments also need to consider the unique characteristics of the school population. If the population is quite different from national norms (e.g., primarily Hispanic), then the school might want to consider developing its own norms. In cases where students are not linguistically fluent, alternative assessments, such as nonverbal tests and performance-based activities, need to be considered.

Assessments also need to be reliable and valid for the purpose of identifying gifted students. Not only do they need to be aligned to the program and the student, but they also need to show that they are not biased against any group, that they will predict student performance in the gifted program, and that they will discriminate between gifted and other students (e.g., validity issues). Moreover, they need to be consistent, or reliable. It's important that a student's performance will not vary dramatically from one testing to the next. Those involved in selecting assessments need to be familiar with the technical aspects of tests and with books or websites that review tests (e.g., Buros Center for Testing [http://www.unl.edu/buros]; Johnsen, 2011). Once the assessments are selected, all staff need to understand the importance of following specific administration instructions and know how to interpret the results (e.g., what scores and performance variations mean).

Finally, schools need to examine how closely their identification procedures follow local, state, and national policies and standards. National standards may be retrieved online from the National Association for Gifted Children or The Association for the Gifted's websites (http://www.nagc.org; http://www.cectag.org). All individuals (e.g., teachers, parents, administrators, counselors, psychologists) who will be involved in identifying students with gifts and talents need to be aware of these policies, procedures, and standards so that the entire identification process is equitable and the students who need services are identified.

Susan K. Johnsen, Ph. D.
Director of Ph.D. Program in Educational Psychology
Director of Gifted Programs
Baylor University

◇◇

Who else can help in the identification process? The school psychologist, counselor, and classroom teacher can share responsibility for assessing the students. Special teachers of music, art, and drama would be key individuals to assess students for talent in the visual and performing arts. Special education teachers can assist in identifying twice-exceptional students. Parents (who really know the child best) can provide valuable information about developmental milestones as well as interests they see occupying the child's time and attention outside of school.

Another expert, Geoffrey Moon, adds information about the importance of casting a wide net in the identification process. He reminds us not to overlook any child, including those from lower socioeconomic backgrounds, children who are twice-exceptional, those who do not speak English as their first language, as well as children from all ethnic and racial groups.

◇◇

SURVIVAL SECRETS FOR IDENTIFYING DIVERSE STUDENTS

Geoffrey Moon

Grade-level proficiency and growth are the conspicuous goals of public education. Gifted students, who are generally proficient or show abundant intellectual potential, require less attention to achieve these goals, and as a result they receive less. Identification is the tool by which advocates say "attention must be paid," and through which they determine what to do next.

Only through robust and fair identification can the awareness of a school system be sufficiently elevated to support appropriate differentiated education for gifted students. This is doubly true for at-risk groups: the highly creative, the intense, those not motivated by school, the quiet ones, and those not taught to reason at home. At-risk students don't fit educators' expectations and are often ignored.

Identification is robust when its procedures are sufficiently reliable and valid to permit a positive result to be trusted across time, when it seldom requires retesting in order to qualify a student, and when a diagnostic profile is produced. It is better to robustly test 15%–20% of a population than to test all students in a limited way (using one test or group of tests), because narrow identification systems do not equip a teacher to make realistic plans for a student. If a student's superior motivation is measured, but her substantial creativity is not, does her teacher know how to keep her motivated? If a student's highest reasoning capacity is with language, is accelerated language arts the appropriate venue for differentiation, when the school doesn't know whether he likes to read? One-dimensional testing inclines a school toward more programmatic, less individualized educational planning, calling into question the student's gifted status, rather than the appropriateness of his or her program, if it doesn't work. Robust assessment answers those questions before they arise.

Fair identification of giftedness allows for diverse stages of development, prior experience, and patterns of gifted performance recognized across cultures. To accommodate stages of development, more attention should be paid to achievement and intrinsic motivation over time (Subotnik & Jarvin, 2005). In the case of disadvantaged learners, scores that are impacted by experience (such as language and reasoning scores) should be compared to adjusted norms (Slocumb, 2000). By constructing a matrix with domains such as language, math, science, social studies, and visual/spatial ability on one dimension, and with Frasier's (1995) Traits, Aptitudes, and Behaviors or Sternberg's (2000) creative, analytic, and practical triarchy on the other, one can simultaneously search for many kinds of giftedness. A lone spike of analytic or creative performance can demonstrate latent ability. A general pattern of strengths across domains evinces global ability. Aptitudes are apparent when strengths align in a domain. Because the weaker performances on that grid constitute opportunities for growth, an individual plan can be quickly formulated to develop the student's talent.

My experience with the diverse gifted students identified using these procedures is that almost all relish the opportunity to learn from published, research-based gifted curriculum and show advanced growth over time. The journey to advanced performance begins with identification that helps diverse gifted students become understood.

Geoffrey Moon, M.A.T.
Coordinator for Gifted Education
Gallup-McKinley County Schools, New Mexico

◇◇

Individualized Education Program (IEP)

An Individualized Education Program, better known as an IEP, is required in states in which gifted children constitute a category of exceptional children. If that is true in your state, you need to learn as much as possible about the IEP. It is possible that the IEP has another name in your state. For example, in Kentucky the IEP is called the Gifted Student Services Plan. No matter the name, the IEP comes with the weight of law. Publications on students with disabilities will help you understand the IEP further, as will your district's gifted and special education coordinators.

Other Points to Remember to Make Identification Defensible

1. *Match the tools.* Identification tools must match the category being identified. For example, you must use an assessment designed to measure creativity if you are identifying students for creative or productive thinking. Aptitude measures are needed for identification of students as intellectually gifted, while achievement assessments will be used for identifying students as gifted in a specific academic area. Identification in the visual and performing arts will necessitate using performance measures and portfolios.

2. *Communicate.* Communicate with children, parents, and other educators so they know what the term *gifted* or *advanced learner* means and does not mean. Take the mystery out of identification and out of being gifted. Make sure that all parties understand differences among learners, including why some students are ready for more advanced learning experiences.

3. *Include diverse students.* Cast a wide net so as to include children who are from lower socioeconomic backgrounds, who are twice-exceptional, who do not have English as their first language, as well as children from all ethnic and racial groups.

4. *Encourage teacher observation.* Educators should be vigilant as they observe children for evidence that they are more advanced than their peers in one or more areas of giftedness or talent. To be a good observer, the teacher must be familiar with characteristics of gifted learners and know that some of these characteristics may appear to be less than desirable (e.g., asking too many questions to suit the teacher, having lots of energy that needs to be channeled in positive ways through engaging learning experiences).

5. *Hold on to your data.* Keep the tests and assessment data, as you may need them later. The assessments could prove useful in the future, so find a filing cabinet that can be locked in which to keep the results of instruments given to students.

6. *Understand why you identify students.* Remember that identification is not an exact science, but the goal of identification is noble—to recognize strengths among children in order to teach them in ways that will allow their full potentials to develop.

7. *Remember that off-level assessments tell you at what level the child can perform.* An off-level assessment is intended for children or young people who are older; therefore, when you administer the off-level assessment and remove the learning ceiling, you can see at what level the child can perform. An example of an off-level assessment is giving the SAT or the ACT to seventh graders as a part of one of the talent searches. That information should be used as a part of the identification process to plan instruction that is a match for the young person's level of readiness.

Evans and Whaley (n.d.) developed the Jot Downs (see Figures 1 and 2) to help teachers look for behaviors among children in their classes in an easy way. The teacher simply records the name of the child in the square with the specific behavior he saw the child demonstrate. Later the teacher could look for names that were noted for patterns she saw among the students in her class.

The first Jot Down included is for general intellectual ability. This is the type of giftedness that people are most likely to think of when they talk about a gifted child. This type of giftedness is also the one that states use if they recognize only one category of giftedness.

Giftedness in a specific academic ability (see Figure 2) does not have to accompany general intellectual giftedness, but it may. A child may be gifted in one specific academic area or in two or more. The young person who is gifted in math or language arts may well be on grade level in the other subject area. It is

General Intellectual Ability Jot Down

Date _____ / _____ / _____
　　　　Mo. 　　Day 　　Yr.

Teacher _____

Grade _____ School _____

Brief description of observed activity: _____

1. As students show evidence of the following characteristics in comparison with age peers, jot their names down in the appropriate box/es.

2. When recommending students for gifted services, use this identification jot down as a reminder of student performances in the area of general intellectual ability.

Sees connections/recognizes patterns; may want to know how what is being taught fits in.	Asks many probing questions, sometimes to the point of driving others up the wall.	Appears to have a deep sense of justice. May correct others when something seems wrong.	Able to work one or more years above others in age group.
Widely read or likes to read. May prefer to read rather than be with others.	Knows many things that have not been taught.	Has a large vocabulary but may choose when to use it.	Benefits from rapid rate of presentation. May refuse to do work seen as busy work.

Figure 1. General intellectual ability jot down. From *Jot downs* by M. A. Evans & L. Whaley (n.d.), unpublished manuscript, The Center for Gifted Studies, Western Kentucky University, Bowling Green, KY. Reprinted with permission of the authors.

Figure 1, continued

Displays intensity for learning. Preoccupied and hard to move on to new topic or area of study.	Prefers a few close friends with similar intellect to many friends.	Has knowledge about things age peers may not be aware of.
Prefers to work independently with little direction. May be resistant to being the leader of a group.	Displays abstract thinking. Requires time to think before responding.	Likes to observe before trying new activities. Thinks through ideas before sharing with others.
	Shows high energy level (physical, intellectual, and psychological).	Appears to have discrepancies between physical, social, and intellectual development.

important to understand that a gifted child may be gifted in various ways. Being gifted may look different in various individuals.

Remember that all student behaviors that indicate giftedness in a specific category are not positive or endearing to the teacher. It is important for teachers to recognize when characteristics of gifted students (like asking many questions or developing areas of deep passion and interest) can be beneficial, despite whether they sometimes present themselves as negative.

• •

Wow . . . I wish I had these over the past 18 years. By reading through the "characteristic traits" on the different Jot Downs, I can think back to students in the past who I probably let slip by because I didn't have the correct perspective of what gifted meant. I had a definition in my head from personal experience with my own child, and that narrows the field for students gifted in other areas. The one thing that will help teachers use these efficiently is the teacher-friendly language of the statements that describe what teachers need to look for in students to jot down. I will definitely share these with the teachers at my school to see if they will facilitate more collaboration between them and our Leap teacher.

Kristi Hayes
Teacher
Bullitt County, KY

• •

Gathering Information

The sole reason for identification is to gather information that will assist educators in providing the services or educational experiences that optimize the development of the gifted student's potential. Teachers are accountable for providing services that enrich and extend learning for the student in the specific area(s) of giftedness in which he is identified.

Identification tools must match the category of giftedness that is being assessed. For example, one does not identify a creative thinker with an intelligence test or a child gifted in science by his leadership activities. The next match must be between the area in which the child was identified and the program or service provided to ensure continuous progress in this area of strength. In order to have defensible services, both matches must be made.

If the state gifted regulations specify the number of measures required to identify a child in any category of giftedness, that sets the minimum number of assessments that district personnel must use when identifying gifted children. It is perfectly okay to use more measures, just not fewer.

Specific Academic Area Jot Down

Brief description of
observed activity: _____

Teacher _____

Check One: ☐ Language Arts   Date ___ / ___ / ___
                ☐ Social Studies   Mo.   Day   Yr.
                ☐ Math
                ☐ Science   Grade ___ School ___

1. As students show evidence of the following characteristics in comparison with age peers, jot their names down in the appropriate box/es.
2. When recommending students for gifted services, use this identification jot down as a reminder of student performances in this specific academic area.

Sees connections.	Asks many probing questions.	Shares what he or she knows, which may be seen as answering "too often."	Provides many written/oral details.
Is widely read or likes to read about the subject area.	Absorbs information quickly from limited exposure.	Has a large vocabulary in subject area.	Benefits from rapid rate of presentation in subject area.

Figure 2. Specific academic area jot down. From *Jot Downs* by M. A. Evans & L. Whaley (n.d.), unpublished manuscript, The Center for Gifted Studies, Western Kentucky University, Bowling Green, KY. Reprinted with permission of the authors.

Figure 2, continued

Displays intensity for learning within subject area.	Requires little or no drill to grasp concepts.	Has knowledge about things age peers may not be aware of.
Prefers to work independently with little direction.	Displays leadership qualities within subject area.	Generates large number of ideas or solutions to problems.
	Applies knowledge to unfamiliar situations.	Offers unusual or unique responses.

Practical Guidelines for Administering Assessments

1. Make certain that conditions are conducive for the children to perform at optimum levels. Do not give the assessment in lieu of going outside for recess or during a favorite activity.
2. Ensure that the children are familiar with a computer if one is being used in the assessment. Do not use any equipment that does not work well or that is unfamiliar to the children.
3. Provide the optimum time required by the assessment to allow the children to do their very best. Assessments can lead to opportunities (e.g., being identified in one or more categories of giftedness, earning a score that qualifies them for outside opportunities).
4. Control the conditions for the assessment to make sure that children are not distracted. Make certain that others will not be calling or knocking on the door and that there are no disruptions to break the students' trains of thought.
5. Practice administering the assessment before it really counts for children.

Perhaps you think that such problems do not occur during the identification process, but they actually do. No one plans on these negative conditions, but letting them occur is poor practice and the result of benign negligence.

Conclusion

Appropriately identifying gifted and talented students is key to ensuring that they receive the educations they need and deserve. It is vital for teachers and administrators to use the best practices outlined in this chapter to identify students from a variety of different backgrounds and talent areas for gifted programming. Using the Jot Downs and remembering the key points to making identification defensible can help you make important decisions about which of your students qualify for gifted programs or services.

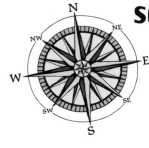

Survival Tips

- Cast a wide net when identifying children as gifted and talented.

- In addition to providing one piece of information for identification, the Jot Downs can provide professional development for teachers as they watch for behaviors that are characteristic of a particular category of giftedness among students in their classes.

O Parents need to have available information about identification so the process is transparent. They also need to know the grievance procedure if they want further steps to be taken in the identification process.

Survival Toolkit

O *Identification of Gifted and Talented* (http://www.youtube.com/watch?v=WjjVTPpimDk&feature=related): This video on identification makes good points about identification in general and then specifically focuses on identification in South Carolina.

O *Instruments Used in the Identification of Gifted and Talented Students* (http://www.gifted.uconn.edu/nrcgt/reports/rm95130/rm95130.pdf): The National Research Center for the Gifted and Talented published the instrument bank found at the above site to aid in the identification of students and the gathering of data.

O Johnsen, S. K. (Ed.). (2011). *Identifying gifted students: A practical guide*. Waco, TX: Prufrock Press.

7 Educators as Talent Developers

Unless you find a child's specific talent—and provide him or her with the exact means needed to express it—it may go undiscovered. (Scheve, 2010, para. 3)

Key Question	
• What must be in place for talent to develop at exceptional levels?	

Athletic coaches look for talent among all young people to ensure that they are getting appropriate opportunities to develop their talents; in other words, they serve as talent scouts for this population. That same aggressive search for talent is not often evident in academics. In fact, talent often goes unnoticed in classrooms, in the hope that variations in ability will not cause more work for the teacher. The focus on reaching proficiency in academics is a noble goal if the child is not there yet, but proficiency is no goal at all for children who are either at the point of proficiency or beyond. Proficiency is grade-level learning. No coach would be satisfied with proficiency as the goal for the players on a varsity team. How can educators do anything less than coaches do in talent development? Teachers and educational leaders must launch a search for talent and then work to develop that talent to its full potential.

Talent development depends on first finding evidence of interest in a talent area. As talent scouts, each educator, counselor, and administrator looks for interests and even passions as the early evidence of talent. It is important not to miss the opportunity to talk with the child about his or her interests and passions. The next step is matching that early sign of interest and/or talent with opportunities. Those opportunities may be contests or competitions, but they may also be putting together a pair or a group of young people who share the interest. It may be cluster-grouping children of similar readiness levels so that they can advance as they are ready to do so. Educators may also consider recommending the child for Saturday or summer programming to help the child find peers.

The Schoolwide Enrichment Model for Talent Development

The Schoolwide Enrichment Model (Renzulli & Reis, 1997) divided learning experiences into three types—Type I, Type II, and Type III. Type I experiences are for all children. They may be a guest speaker, a field trip, a video, or any other opportunity to expose the students to a new idea, topic, or career. There is no expectation that all children will be motivated to move on with that topic, but the experience may spark the interest of one or more of the young people. Type II activities build skills. These skills may be critical and creative thinking skills, problem-solving skills, technical skills, research skills, or skills needed for specific products. Type III activities are for students who have an idea that they want to investigate in depth.

One expert, Sally Reis, discusses the importance of passion in developing lifelong interests. Often the topic that develops into a passion begins in an independent study, and Dr. Reis shares some examples of this in action through the use of the Schoolwide Enrichment Model.

SURVIVAL SECRETS ON THE ROLE OF PASSION IN TALENT DEVELOPMENT

Sally Reis

I have recently spent some time thinking about passion areas and how students both develop and sustain them. Over the last few years, I have been in contact with several former gifted and talented students from the school district in which I taught and coordinated the gifted program. All of these young people participated in the gifted program in our district that was based on Joseph Renzulli's original Enrichment Triad Model. For example, I received an e-mail from a student who worked with me during elementary school in our Triad gifted and talented program. Sherry e-mailed and told me that she had recently completed her Ph.D. in science and would be at the University of Connecticut giving a symposium in her area of expertise: pharmaceutical chemistry.

It was the note that she sent that caused me to smile: She wrote indicating that it was the projects she had finished in our Triad program that caused her to want to continue to pursue her Ph.D. She explained that in her years of doing Type III independent studies, she had learned to be passionate about her work from her earliest experiences doing projects and solving problems. In three related instances, I heard from other students from this elementary school who participated in our gifted program and subsequently completed a law degree, a doctoral degree in counseling, and medical school. What did I learn from my former students?

I learned that my students explored their interests and developed their passions over time. In their early years, they explored and developed their childhood interests. As they grew older, their interests and academic talents merged with work and subsequent career interests, enabling them to explore academic paths in areas of passion and finally to help them find work in careers as adult creative producers.

My colleague and friend, Thomas Hébert, and I have talked about this over time, and we believe that our former students developed some of their passion because of their gifted program involvement. For example, their in-depth Type III interests often affected their college majors and their careers. In a favorite example, Tom followed up on four students who had worked on a Type III project in an elementary school Triad program he called "Bobby Bones." These students built a skeletal model of the human body and created a video-based learning module to teach anatomy that accompanied the skeleton when it visited various classrooms. The students who worked on this project were all interested in anatomy, and Tom later learned that three of these four students finished medical school. Tom interviewed these students, who told him that they believed that their Type III project served as important training for later productivity. I have heard from many of my former students who said that their Type III projects served as life-shaping influences on college and their careers, and also as the basis of their subsequent motivation and continued desire for creative outlets throughout their education and life. They also told me that these interest-based projects consistently enhanced very special nonintellectual characteristics such as task commitment, curiosity, and creativity.

So, in my experience, passion develops from involvement in creative projects, the opportunity to explore and play with early interests, the chance to become creative producers, and the opportunity to solve problems in areas of personal interest. Imagine the world we could have if talented and gifted students from across the globe were able to choose important problems and issues, a goal of Type III enrichment, and try to solve them in their life work. I believe that these things are possible if students are able to identify, develop, and explore their interests, and subsequently to find work that is based on their passions.

Sally Reis, Ph.D.
Board of Trustees Distinguished Professor
University of Connecticut

Other Avenues for Talent Development

Educators play a huge role in talent development, and parents do as well. Parents need to share information about their child's interests with teachers and seek opportunities for their child to be with others who share his interests. For example, an 8-year-old chess player may not find other age-mates who love chess in his class or school, and a budding artist may need to find classes after school or on Saturdays to see that she has opportunities for continuing to develop her artistic talent. It is difficult for a child to be the only one of her peers with a particular interest. It is worth the extra effort for parents to find soulmates for their children, so they can continue to pursue their interests and realize that other young people love doing what they also love. Summer camps for academics and the arts afford opportunities for students to find other young people who share their interests and goals.

Expert Rena Subotnik sets the stage for you to see talent development as something that doesn't just happen, but rather is the result of persistence and dedication.

SURVIVAL SECRETS FOR PSYCHOLOGICAL STRENGTH TRAINING AND TALENT DEVELOPMENT

Rena Subotnik

In 1962, Abraham Tannenbaum discovered that students admired "brilliant" classmates as long as they were also athletic and *not studious*. That is, they didn't show signs of actually having to put in effort to achieve their brilliance. Even 50 years later, this notion of spontaneous brilliance leads many capable children to avoid taking on challenges that require extra work so as to avoid looking dumb. My colleagues and I have derived some solutions to this conundrum from the worlds of elite music and sport. Both domains have invested attention into ensuring that the children and youth who have potential to excel receive not only good physical skills and technique training, but also practice in *mental skills*. Athletes and musicians strive for the appearance of effortlessness, yet know that the way they get there is through guided practice and persistent effort. Unfortunately, these lessons have not yet been widely adopted in classrooms with elite *academic* performers.

What are some of the mental skills that coaches share with athletes and musicians? A central message is to view adversity as part of the "game," and part of life—you can't allow setbacks to rattle you too much, and each setback provides an insight into improvement for next time. Second, athletes and musicians are more productive if they compare their current efforts with their own past performance, rather than making comparisons to others, and always strive to reach aspired personal goals.

At music conservatories, mental skills training varies with students' levels of expertise. For example, in the early stages of professional training, it's important to support novice musicians' willingness to practice what their teachers identify as their weaknesses, even when they've been praised effusively for how they already performed when they entered the conservatory. After students acquire a degree of expertise, teachers expect their students to take on more responsibility for identifying and addressing their own strengths and weaknesses. At the most advanced stages of talent development, emerging musical artists capitalize primarily on their strengths while shoring up weaknesses as needed. With each advancing stage, students must exercise increasing amounts of responsibility and risk taking in order to develop abilities into competencies, expertise, and then artistry.

At sport and music institutions, specialized coaches and teachers provide instruction in these mental skills, or what we call "psychological strength training." Classroom teachers can fulfill some of this role by carefully considering their use of praise. You can compliment students for taking a risk intellectually, tackling their weak skills with vigor, accepting successes gracefully, and being a good sport about other people's accomplishments. Most important is for teachers to model how to handle the fact that most days involve setbacks as well as accomplishment.

The principles of psychological strength training are based on good science. They work to improve students' productivity and yours, too.

Rena Subotnik, Ph.D.
Director, Center for Psychology in Schools and Education, and Associate Executive Director, Education Directorate
American Psychological Association

Benjamin Bloom on Talent Development

In talent development, it is important to capture interest and then to continue the talent development process on an ongoing basis. Bloom (1985), in his study of talent development among internationally eminent people, made the following statement:

No matter how precocious one is at age ten or eleven, if the individual doesn't stay with the talent development process over many years, he or she will soon be outdistanced by others who do continue. A long-term commitment to the talent field and an increasing passion for talent development are essential if the individual is to attain the highest levels of capability in the field. Natural talent or high interest may be the starting places in talent development, but it is the long-term commitment that will sustain progress in an area of talent. (p. 538)

Bloom clearly made the point that a young person must have ongoing opportunities to develop any talent that he has or he will not develop his talent at the same levels as others who stay involved. In other words, unless a student sticks with the talent area, she will not develop her full potential.

Malcolm Gladwell on Talent Development

Malcolm Gladwell (2008) noted in his popular book *The Outliers: The Story of Success* that it takes 10,000 hours of practice in a talent area in order to perform at a truly outstanding level. Discovering talent is only the starting point in talent development. As Gladwell stated, "But what truly distinguishes their histories is not their extraordinary talent but their extraordinary opportunities" (p. 11). Teachers can help gifted young people access the opportunities they need to develop their talents.

NAGC's Redefining Giftedness

Recently, NAGC (2010b) issued a statement entitled *Redefining Giftedness for a New Century: Shifting the Paradigm* (see http://www.nagc.org/index.aspx?id=6404&terms=Redefining+giftedness). It added a talent development focus to terminology in gifted education:

> The development of ability or talent is a lifelong process. It can be evident in young children as exceptional performance on tests and/or other measures of ability, or as a rapid rate of learning, compared to other students of the same age, or in actual achievement in a domain. As individuals mature through childhood to adolescence, however, achievement and high levels of motivation in the domain become the primary characteristics of their giftedness. Various factors can either enhance or inhibit the development and expression of abilities. (para. 2)

Conclusion

So why should you be interested in talent development? The reasons are numerous, but let's start out with a very important one. You create your future when you ensure that children who are gifted and talented are appropriately challenged. Educating your students to actualize their potentials will assure your future.

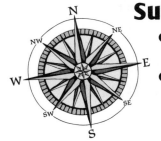

Survival Tips

- Educators must see being a talent scout as an important role.

- Parents need to know that academic and artistic talents follow a similar pattern as athletic talent. Interest may be sparked early, often before their children's age-mates have that interest. Then, their children need teachers who develop their skills at the next higher level on an ongoing basis. Levels of learning and performance are not limited by the age of the young person.

Survival Toolkit

- Bloom, B. S. (1985). *Developing talent in young people*. New York, NY: Ballantine.

- Csikzentmihalyi, M., Rathunde, K., & Whalen, S. (1996). *Talented teenagers: The roots of success and failure*. New York, NY: Cambridge University Press.

- Jarvin, L., & Subotnik, R. F. (2005). Understanding elite talent in academic domains: A developmental trajectory from basic abilities to scholarly productivity/artistry. In F. Dixon & S. Moon (Eds.), *The handbook of secondary gifted education* (pp. 203–220). Waco, TX: Prufrock Press.

- Neihart, M. (2008). *Peak performance for smart kids: Strategies and tips for ensuring school success*. Waco, TX: Prufrock Press.

- Van Yperen, N. W. (2009). Why some make it and others do not: Identifying psychological factors that predict career success in professional adult soccer. *The Sport Psychologist, 23*, 317–329.

8 Maximizing Potential Through Social and Emotional Understanding and Support

The most common counseling need of this [gifted] population is assistance in coping with stressors related to growing up as a gifted child in a society that does not always recognize, understand, or welcome giftedness.—Sidney M. Moon

Key Question

- What should you know about the social and emotional development of children and young people who are gifted and talented?

Many people have the misperception that gifted children must be as socially awkward as Sheldon Cooper on the television show *The Big Bang Theory*. Not true. When young people who are gifted and talented have opportunities to interact with others who share their interests, they are remarkably social. It is when they cannot find others to talk with about mutual interests that they may appear less than social. That, however, is a problem for most people who find it difficult to appear social when they find they have nothing to talk about with others—nothing of mutual interest. Just consider what it is like for someone who has no interest in the Super Bowl when it is Super Bowl Sunday and that sporting event is the topic of conversation in many, if not most, circles. The social-emotional development of gifted children is nurtured or stunted by so many things in their lives. You must learn about their social-emotional development in order to support the development of their potential.

Gifted Children's Bill of Rights

A way to establish a classroom and a school in which all children who are gifted and talented thrive is to understand what it takes for them to do so. In 2008, Del Siegle, then president of the National Association for Gifted Children, presented the organization's membership with the Gifted Children's Bill of Rights (see Figure 3), which makes important suggestions. Each statement will provide sage guidance to you as a teacher, whether you have one gifted child or an entire classroom of gifted children. Posting the Bill of Rights in your classroom is a good reminder of key tenets that create a positive classroom environment. The Bill of Rights is also important to share with parents and the students themselves. When teachers and parents convey similar messages to their children, young people are the winners.

Two Sets of Peers for Gifted Children

Understanding the needs of gifted children includes knowing that they have two sets of peers—their age-mates and their intellectual peers (those with whom they share an interest or a passion). Intellectual peers are often, but not always, older children. Gifted children find that because they share interests with their intellectual peers, it is easy to talk with them and create friendships. One reason to provide grouping for instructional purposes is to allow children to find age-mates who are also intellectual peers. Every person needs someone with whom they relate easily, and gifted children are no exception. It is very lonely for a child to be in a classroom in which he can't find anyone else who is interested in anything about which he is passionate. "What's wrong with me?" can be the concern when a child feels isolated. Of course, being different can be positive, but to many children and adolescents, being different does not bring about positive feelings.

Grouping for instructional purposes can go a long way toward ensuring that children have peers for discussion, intellectual stimulation, and encouragement. Those potential groupings can focus on interests, readiness, or needs. They can be short-term for a project or flexible groupings. They can be cluster groups or homogeneous classes.

Sometimes children find kindred spirits in activities outside the school. Musical and sporting opportunities, as well as organizations of various types, can lead to finding peers who share interests. Saturday and summer programs also provide opportunities for children to find others with whom they can easily relate. Author Barbara Kingsolver (2002) wrote that her daughter's experience at

Gifted Children's Bill of Rights

You have a right . . .

1 . . . to know about your giftedness.

2 . . . to learn something new every day.

3 . . . to be passionate about your talent area without apologies.

4 . . . to have an identity beyond your talent area.

5 . . . to feel good about your accomplishments.

6 . . . to make mistakes.

7 . . . to seek guidance in the development of your talent.

8 . . . to have multiple peer groups and a variety of friends.

9 . . . to choose which of your talent areas you wish to pursue.

10 . . . not to be gifted at everything.

—Del Siegle
2007–2009 NAGC President

NATIONAL ASSOCIATION FOR
Gifted Children
http://www.nagc.org

Provided as a service of
the National Association for Gifted Children & Prufrock Press Inc.
Copies are available online at http://www.nagc.org

PRUFROCK PRESS INC.
The Nation's Leading Resource for Gifted and Advanced Learners
http://www.prufrock.com

Figure 3. Gifted children's bill of rights. From National Association for Gifted Children (http://www.nagc.org). Reprinted with permission.

a summer program for gifted young people "helped her understand the potential rewards of belonging to a peer group that's more interested in Jane Austen and Shakespeare than Calvin Klein and Tommy Hilfiger" (p. 9).

Gifted Children as a Diverse Population

Gifted children are a very diverse population. They share many, but not all, characteristics. They tend to be at the extremes on some characteristics. For example, they tend to be very well organized or not very well organized at all. Many show intensities in their behaviors. Whereas all children are curious, gifted children may exhibit a curiosity that seems like nonstop questioning. Intensities are fairly typical among gifted young people.

Children who are gifted and talented often develop very specific interests at an early age. Zach may become so interested in dinosaurs that everything he wants to read or to have you read relates to dinosaurs. Elizabeth may develop her interest in history by playing with her American Girl doll Felicity and wanting to read all of the books that are available about Felicity and the time she represents. Jose may be very, very interested in playing chess before anyone else in his class shares that interest. Or Caroline may want to learn all about butterflies, even though no one knows where she got that fascination. The key is for students to find others who share the interest (idea-mates or older students) to keep the child learning about a topic that she finds so very interesting. Do not worry—the interest will likely shift to a new topic about which she will have a similar intensity to learn.

Expert Thomas P. Hébert shares his thoughts and strategies for addressing the social and emotional needs of children who are gifted and talented. He describes strategies that you will find both enjoyable and useful to implement.

◇◇

SURVIVAL SECRETS ON MEETING THE SOCIAL AND EMOTIONAL DEVELOPMENT OF GIFTED STUDENTS
Thomas P. Hébert

Meg's parents were facing a divorce, and she appreciated my spending time after school listening to her express her fears about how her family would change. Molly, an elementary student, released the bees trapped in her jelly jar following our trip to a beekeeper's farm because she could not emotionally deal with seeing them trapped. Andrew joined me for brown bag lunches and important man-to-man conversations about his struggles to find other middle school boys who appreciated his intelligence, sensitivity, and creativity. As an educator, I have been blessed with opportunities to teach a variety of student populations, and through my experiences with students like Meg, Molly, and Andrew, I have learned how important it is to understand what is happening in young people's lives beyond my classroom. The more I worked with highly intelligent students, the more I realized the importance of understanding their social and emotional lives.

Today, in my university classroom, I work with graduate students and educators to pay close attention to particular social and emotional characteristics and behaviors evidenced in gifted learners. I call attention to the following characteristics to assist them in understanding gifted students (Hébert, 2011):

- high expectations of self and others (perfectionism);
- internal motivation, inner locus of control;
- emotional sensitivity, intensity, and depth;
- empathy;
- advanced levels of moral maturity with consistency between values and actions;
- strong need for self-actualization;
- highly developed sense of humor; and
- resilience.

With an understanding that gifted students often display these characteristics, educators realize that these characteristics may influence their childhood and adolescent development in different ways. To assist gifted students in their developmental journey, it is critical that educators create supportive classroom cultures. In my work with graduate students and teachers in gifted education, I spend much time addressing how to create a healthy emotional climate in a classroom. My goal is to have teachers design environments that enable young people to feel valued for their intelligence and creativity, and respected as individuals by both their teacher and classmates. The following strategies are three favorites that I implemented in my classroom to support the social and emotional development of my students. My hope is that my readers will consider incorporating them in their own classroom practice.

Business Cards

During the first week of school, I facilitated an activity I called "Business Cards." I explained to my students how professionals have business cards that present an image to the world of what they are all about. I then shared with them my collection of business cards and pointed out how many of them send a clear message. I have collected cards from all over the country and have enjoyed showing students how Ann Marie McGranaghan's card from "The Courtesy Cleaning Company" in Bowling Green, OH, speaks to me with its clean crisp lines that say Anne Marie offers a housecleaning service that is thorough and fussy—the kind of woman I would want taking care of my home. My card from "Cakes Extraordinaire" in Portland, ME, is a simple and elegant-looking card. I decided to order my parents' 50th wedding anniversary cake from this bakery because I wanted a cake that was simple and elegant looking. It was a smart decision. The cake I ordered was perfect and made a big hit on my parents' special day.

After the introduction of my card collection, I had students reflect on the question "What does a business card say about you?" I distributed large sheets of construction paper and provided them time to design their personal business cards. My objective behind this activity was to have gifted students find a friend. I wanted the science fiction buffs to find each other. I wanted the Boston Red Sox fans to find other sports enthusiasts. I wanted the girls who designed step dance routines to find other dancers and to have the computer experts discover each other. The business cards were prominently displayed on the walls of my classroom, common interests were recognized, and children were able to make friendship connections. This nonthreatening activity was what I needed to begin building community and supportive relationships.

A Classroom Mailbox

I incorporated a classroom mailbox that enabled students to communicate with me privately. I covered a box with brightly colored contact paper and announced to my students that if they were to leave a letter in my mailbox, I would guarantee that they would find a letter from me the next day in a sealed envelope. Many of the letters I received were enjoyable and helpful to me in understanding what my students were thinking about their experiences in my classroom. More important to me were the letters I received that were calls for help. "Dear Mr. Hébert, my mom and dad are getting a divorce. They want me to decide who I want to live with. Can you help me decide? Your student, Dustin." I responded to Dustin's note the next day with a private conversation and an explanation of the special training Mrs. Jones, our school counselor, had undergone in order to be able to help children who faced such situations. I introduced Dustin to Mrs. Jones that day and made certain he spent time with her during this difficult period. The classroom mailbox became an important outlet for students to share their personal lives with me when they needed support or a significant adult to listen to what was on their minds.

Guiding Students to Self-Understanding Through Literature

I have long been a proponent of using literature to facilitate discussions with students about their issues or concerns. I believe that authentic interactions with literature contribute to affective growth. In facilitating good discussions with young people about good books, teachers can help them draw parallels between their experiences and those of the main characters in the books. During such discussions, the students have an opportunity to listen to their classroom peers as they share their feelings about personal experiences related to the focus of the lesson. Such an approach is an attempt to help gifted students understand themselves and cope with problems by providing literature relevant to their developmental needs at appropriate times. In any discussion of high-quality literature with young people, the goal is to have participants share their feelings and listen closely to each other as well as to themselves. In such a conversation, it is important that students leave the classroom with an awareness that others have experienced the same feelings. With the guidance of an empathic teacher, a group discussion can bring about an understanding that "we are in this together." After discussing the book, teachers then incorporate meaningful and enjoyable follow-up activities such as artistic responses, creative writing, journaling, writing song lyrics, writing raps, designing television commercials, or other self-selected options for students to pursue individually or collaboratively. As students engage in these activities, conversations continue and students provide each other with supportive feedback.

Through these three classroom strategies, I gained many important insights about my students. These simple and non-threatening methods enabled me to come to know them as gifted young people, and in our work together I was better prepared to support their social and emotional development. I encourage my readers to do the same.

Thomas P. Hébert, Ph.D.
University of Georgia

◇◇◇

A Few Strategies That Address Social-Emotional Development

There are many ideas you can implement to provide a positive classroom environment for all children. One such strategy is to have a place in the classroom for children to go to "escape" for some quiet time. That place could be a rug in the corner of the room, a beanbag, or a pillow on the floor. Although those suggestions sound more applicable to an elementary classroom, it is also appropriate for older students to have a quiet space. Perhaps a pass to the library could offer a few minutes to escape if such time were needed.

Choice is also a strategy that recognizes the strengths, interests, and passions of gifted young people. Of course, choice is not always appropriate, but occasionally students can be offered choice of a topic (the content), the way they will pursue the topic cognitively (the process), and the way they will demonstrate what they have learned (the product). Think of the positive social-emotional climate that is created when students have opportunities for differentiated learning experiences. There is an important tie between the social-emotional development of a child and the opportunities she has or does not have to learn new content and develop her thinking on a day-to-day basis. The following poem by a gifted young person can help you to see her wishes for learning.

· ·

Stop Holding Us Back

You wouldn't tell a bird
Not to fly
You wouldn't tell a baby
Not to cry
So why
Do you keep holding
Me back?

You wouldn't tell
The wind not to blow
Or a river not to flow
Or the waves in the ocean
Not to crash
But you keep telling me
That you don't believe
In my potential
Oh why
Do you keep holding me back?

You wouldn't tell a star
Not to shine
Or the sun
Not to rise
Don't you realize
You're holding me back?

You're resisting what should be
And it's not hurting just me
So I'm asking you please
Just see what you're doing

Here in us lies such great potential
Such potential for so many great things
And I say to you
We ARE the future
That's what I'm trying to make you see

And you, yes you
Are building your future
And I know you hope
It will be a great one
But the future is only ensured by the present
And presently, let's look
At all that you've done

Raise us up
For we are the next leaders
Don't stifle us
Hear what we must say
Push us
Because we are tomorrow's thinkers
Don't hold us back
That's not the way
To ensure your bright future
That you hope for
Yes, I know you want one

But for tomorrow's bright future
Today you must teach us
You must let us learn
You must hear us
And believe in us
And I promise
We WILL get more done

Elizabeth Gatten
Ninth grader from Union County, KY

• •

Bullying

A problem that often touches gifted children is bullying. Gifted children are vulnerable to bullying for a couple of reasons. One reason is that many gifted children are especially sensitive. Another reason is that they are often different from their age-mates in their interests and may not have others who share their interests. Being different can make a gifted child the target for a bully. One expert, Brad Tassell, discusses bullying with young people who are gifted and talented.

◇◇

SURVIVAL SECRETS FOR DEALING WITH BULLYING

Brad Tassell

"Why are my friends so mean to me?" a trembling 12-year-old girl asks after my program on bullying at a Northern Indiana school. "They are always making fun of my writing."

Being gifted doesn't mean you aren't confused. It doesn't mean that putting together the idiosyncrasies of complex adolescent relationships is a walk in the park. I had just met a gifted young lady. She was 12 years old, and writing on a level that would make author Christopher Paolini (who wrote *Eragon* at 15) feel like a late bloomer. Cathy was a poet. She read me a few of her poems. Her imagery and pathos were insightful and beautiful. Cathy was confused because every time she would show her "friends" her poems, they would make fun of them, and especially painful, give her no feedback on the depth of her poetic vision. They couldn't even understand the meter, for heaven's sake! Did I mention she was 12?

Cathy couldn't understand what it is very easy for us to see, but what we rarely help our gifted students realize. Her friends are the real 12. The "normal" 12. The mad-because they-can't-watch-MTV 12. The "OMG, when will my mom let me wear makeup?" 12. She is the extraordinary, brilliant 12, and she would need to learn to use that difference to her advantage, not disadvantage.

I asked Cathy how her friends treated her at other times, and she said, "Fine." They hung out at school, went to movies, and so forth. Yet whenever she asked anyone in her town to read her poems, the eyes would start to roll.

My advice to Cathy, and to my own daughter whose intellectual interest runs close to seven grade levels above those of her peers, was simple. Stop showing them the poetry. "Third graders can't see the corporate microcosm humor related in Dilbert," I said to my confused daughter one day. I told Cathy how beautiful her work was, but that her friends won't understand, and that she was "feeding the bully" by continuing to show it to them. That doesn't make them bad or her work less genius. Gifted kids want people, especially their peers, to share their passions, but many times get bullied for their intelligence and intensity. Parents can help them in a few positive ways:

1. Be a champion for their gift. My daughter at 8 is very deep into Greek mythology. I listen hard to every second of it. I am engrossed. I want to hear her talk about it, even though it may not be something I would chose to learn on my own.
2. Help them learn the cues that others are not interested. It's sad, but nobody in her third-grade class is going to want to know the difference between a cerberus and a chimera, and continuing to force it on them will cause pain. Learning to read signals from others is a very good life skill.

Gifted students often feel isolated. Cathy felt like the alien from Planet Thoreau. My advice to her might help someone you know. Let them know:

1. Your people are out there. You might have to get to college first, but they are there. Parents can help their children today by finding safe places online or others who share their passion.
2. Your gift can be isolating now, but don't let it isolate you. It's good to learn how to deal with peers on their level. Parents, help your gifted learner understand that the needs of others are important, too, and it's not always about their own ideas and interests.

Cathy had a nice epiphany and said she would probably take my advice. Bullying for gifted kids can be lessened by helping them understand the message, *Don't Feed the Bully*. Help them understand that they are brilliant, but that brilliance is not universal to their classmates. Help them find positive feedback for their great gifts; then, like Cathy, have poetry and an ice cream party, too.

Brad Tassell
Author of *Don't Feed the Bully*, Llessat Publishing
Bowling Green, KY

◇◇

Counseling Gifted Students

Bullying is only one of the issues that young people face at all levels of schooling. Teachers, counselors, and principals can work together to create a positive climate in schools, including helping students see the dangers in bullying and working with students to build self-esteem. People with positive self-concepts have fewer needs to take advantage of others.

In order to have social-emotional needs addressed, the counselor plays a key role. It is important that counselors have accurate information about gifted children and their needs in order to facilitate the development of their potentials. Expert Jean Peterson describes the counselor's responsibilities with young people who are gifted and talented.

SURVIVAL SECRETS ON THE ROLE OF COUNSELORS IN GIFTED EDUCATION

Jean Peterson

Counseling focuses largely on normal developmental challenges. Counseling recognizes pathology, but typically focuses on affirming personal strengths, empowering people to make changes, problem solving, coping with transitions, or exploring complex feelings.

Giftedness does not preclude social and emotional difficulties, and counselors can not only validate and normalize feelings, but also help gifted youth to make sense of themselves, feel heard, and develop effective coping strategies. All gifted individuals face universal developmental challenges; however, how they experience development may be qualitatively different from how others experience it. Nevertheless, developmental challenges may not come to mind when educators consider services for gifted students. Educators and even parents may believe that only academic challenge is needed. If academic performance or nonperformance is the main or only focus, "normal development" might not be discussed much at home or school. Gifted students themselves tend to be reluctant to ask for help, according to my research. Therefore, when social and emotional development is not formally a program focus, school counselors may have little contact with gifted high school students other than when the latter need assistance with schedules and college applications.

The asset side of giftedness can indeed help highly able youth cope with difficulties. Intelligence is always on lists of factors of resilience. In contrast, the burden side may be reflected in expressed or unexpressed emotional reactivity, unrelentingly rapid information processing, a lack of support from adults or peers, heavy responsibilities, unreasonable expectations from self and others, and high stress. Adults, peers, and even family may assume that giftedness means being able to cope with anything.

Characteristics associated with giftedness, such as sensitivity, overexcitability, and intensity, may be pathologized by professionals and dismissed by peers as simply "weird." When school and community counselors understand how giftedness can potentially exacerbate challenges related to developmental and other transitions, gifted students are likely to feel understood and to make sense of confusing feelings and behaviors. When counselors are respectful of the asset-burden paradox, they are likely able to build a therapeutic alliance with gifted children and teens.

School counselors, through large- or small-group work, can help both high-academic achievers and underachievers connect meaningfully with each other, develop social skills, learn to express emotions effectively and appropriately, and find support. Counselors can attend to career development, including with young gifted children, who often are precociously concerned about their multipotentiality and the future. Perfectionism, procrastination, anxiety, fears, self-image, and concerns about college life are among topics that can be discussed, as well as developmental concerns related to identity and differentiating from family. Counselors can offer a nonjudgmental presence, poised and thoughtful reflection, validation of "humanness," and a crucial respite in a competitive school environment.

School counselors are capable of conducting individual sessions, but typically are responsible for several hundred students, limiting time for regular, extended clinical work. When a gifted student's feelings or behaviors are significantly affecting relationships, well-being, and the work of being a student, a school counselor can offer suggestions for what to look for in community services, including professionals especially trained to work with families.

Jean Sunde Peterson, Ph.D.
Coordinator of the School Counseling Program
Purdue University

Conclusion

Understanding the social and emotional development of gifted children is so important for parents and educators. It is essential for gifted young people to find idea-mates who may or may not be their age-peers. Finding others who share their interests is most likely to happen when students are grouped for instructional purposes as well as in Saturday and summer programs. Teachers and counselors need to understand that gifted young people constitute a diverse group and that removing the learning ceiling is the best way for these exceptional young people to develop their interests and make continuous progress.

Survival Tips

- Never miss an opportunity to tell a student about a strength he has, something that she does well, or a kindness he has displayed. Your comments may inspire your students to soar.

- Parents need to have resources to better understand the social-emotional development of their children.

Survival Toolkit

- *I Am Gifted* (http://www.youtube.com/watch?v=Omx_iLtMjZA&feature=related): This is a Youtube video that you might want to discuss with your students who have been identified as gifted.

- *Supporting Emotional Needs of the Gifted* (SENG; http://www.sengifted.org): The website for this organization has lots *of articles on topics related to the social and emotional development of children who are gifted and talented.*

- Cross, T. L. (2011). *On the social and emotional lives of gifted children* (4th ed.). Waco, TX: Prufrock Press.

- Fonseca, C. (2010). *Emotional intensity in gifted students: Helping kids cope with explosive feelings.* Waco, TX: Prufrock Press.

- Fonseca, C. (2011). *101 success secrets for gifted kids.* Waco, TX: Prufrock Press.

- Galbraith, J. (2009). *The gifted kids' survival guide: For ages 10 & under* (3rd ed.). Minneapolis, MN: Free Spirit.

- Hébert, T. P. (2011). *Understanding the social and emotional lives of gifted students.* Waco, TX: Prufrock Press.

- Peterson, J. S. (2008). *The essential guide to talking with gifted teens: Ready-to-use discussions about identity, stress, relationships, and more.* Minneapolis, MN: Free Spirit.

9 Acceleration: Accommodating a Different Pace for Learning

Schools pay lip-service to the proposition that students should learn at their own pace; in reality, for countless highly able children the pace of their progress through school is determined by the rate of progress of their classmates.—Colangelo, Assouline, & Gross (2004, p. 1)

Key Question	
• What must be in place to make various types of acceleration successful?	

The 18 Types of Acceleration

Acceleration has many forms, only one of which is grade acceleration. Strange as it may seem, most people think that a reference to acceleration automatically means grade skipping. However, the full range of acceleration includes many options (see Figure 4). The key for all forms of acceleration is to make a match between the needs of the child and the acceleration option. After all, the goal is for each child to make continuous progress.

Types of Acceleration

- Early admission to kindergarten
- Early admission to first grade
- Grade skipping
- Continuous progress
- Self-paced instruction
- Subject-matter acceleration/partial acceleration
- Combined classes
- Curriculum compacting
- Telescoping the curriculum
- Mentoring
- Extracurricular programs
- Correspondence courses/distance learning programs
- Early graduation
- Concurrent/dual enrollment
- Advanced Placement
- Credit by examination
- Acceleration in college
- Early entrance into middle school, high school, or college

Figure 4. Types of acceleration. From Southern and Jones (2004).

A Nation Deceived: How Schools Hold Back America's Brightest Students (Colangelo et al., 2004) defined acceleration as "an educational intervention that moves students through an educational program at a faster-than-usual rate or younger-than-typical age" (p. 1). The authors presented a strong case for acceleration, reporting that "(1) the research on acceleration is expansive and consistent; and (2) we are not aware of any other educational practice that is so well researched yet so rarely implemented" (p. 11). Please note that this two-volume series is available at http://www.nationdeceived.org, and within it readers can find a plethora of information on the 18 types of acceleration shown in Figure 4.

These 18 types of acceleration can be divided into two categories—one involves timing of when the child is accelerated and the other relates to the curriculum. Acceleration options that relate to timing include early entry into kindergarten, first grade, middle school, high school, or college. Acceleration options that focus on curricular interventions include self-paced instruction, subject-matter acceleration, mentoring, Advanced Placement classes, and curriculum compacting. Acceleration should be matched to the individual, addressing the needs of the student, so it is important for you to be familiar with all of the options for acceleration.

Acceleration: Opportunities and Barriers

A major barrier to offering appropriate acceleration options is lack of information that many well-meaning people have about accelerating students. So many people knew a person who experienced some type of acceleration and say that it was not a good experience for that person. What parents and educators need to know is that research supports all types of acceleration if the decisions are made carefully by considering the child and matching the opportunity for acceleration to the child.

Another barrier is that many educators only think of whole-grade acceleration (or grade skipping) when the term *acceleration* is used. Whole-grade acceleration can work well, but it is not the only way to accelerate. Other acceleration options should be tried before moving a child up in grade levels.

A young person who is gifted in a specific academic area will need single-subject acceleration. This type of acceleration could involve the child being placed in a cluster group with other children who are similarly advanced in mathematics or by having the child go to a higher grade for math instruction. At the middle school and high school levels, the young person who is ready to progress in math at a faster pace than his age-mates needs opportunities to take more challenging classes. Perhaps he will be taking Algebra I in seventh grade rather than eighth grade. Please remember that there is plenty of math to learn, so don't be discouraged when a well-meaning person remarks, "What will we do when she is a senior or when she runs out of math classes to take?" A far more important question is "How can we be sure that she has every opportunity to learn in math on a continuous basis?" Possibilities for extending learning include virtual math classes or college classes. It is also possible for the high school to add more advanced math options to the curriculum.

The acceleration option that a particular child needs may be offered solely at another building. In that case, who is responsible for providing transportation when the child needs to take a class at the middle school but is still in the elementary grades, or is in middle school but needs to go to the high school for one or more classes? Often a parent takes the child to the class (which hopefully has been arranged to be during the first or last period slot so that time is not used for transportation on both sides of the class). The preferable solution for transporting children to classes in other buildings is for the district to assume the responsibility. That way, more children can participate when they demonstrate readiness for the more advanced opportunities. If the district assumes responsibility for transporting students to a different school, children whose parents could not provide rides would not be kept from learning at an accelerated pace. It will be important to find out what the policies are in your school district.

Another way to accelerate is to have children start school at a younger age. In cases in which the child demonstrates readiness to enter kindergarten early, doing so may or may not be possible. The answer would depend on the law in the state and/or policy in the school district. In some states, a child who demonstrates readiness to move to a higher grade will be easy to accelerate, while other states throw up a barrier by requiring that a child must be 5 years old by August 1 or September 15. With deadlines for starting school, it is very desirable to have an option for assessing the readiness of individual children whose birthdays do not fall within the published deadline.

Still another way to accelerate students is for them to enter a school earlier than their age-mates. For example, early entrance to college is one way to move through school at a faster pace than anticipated. This option includes matriculating into college ahead of schedule. It could also mean going to a residential school that specializes in mathematics and science in which the students complete high school while they are earning 2 years of college credit. The Carol Martin Gatton Academy of Mathematics and Science in Kentucky (http://www.wku/academy) is one example of this acceleration possibility.

Making Whole-Grade Acceleration the Right Choice

When a full-grade skip is thought to be the best way to meet a child's academic needs, assessment is in order. The child and the receiving teacher must be on board for a grade acceleration to work. The third edition of the *Iowa Acceleration Scale* (Assouline, Colangelo, Lupkowski-Shoplik, Forstadt, & Lipscomb, 2009) is a useful tool to guide your decision making. A point to remember about a grade skip is that advancing the child will only solve the problem for a short time, and differentiation and other acceleration strategies will be also needed. After all, a child who is grade accelerated is usually achieving at two or more levels above his current grade, so skipping a grade may be a temporary solution that will need various adjustments if the child is to make continuous progress.

Have an Acceleration Policy in Place

Having policy in place is very important for addressing children's needs for any type of acceleration. The Institute for Research and Policy on Acceleration's *Guidelines for Developing an Academic Acceleration Policy* can be found at http://www.accelerationinstitute.org/Resources/Policy_Guidelines. It is always good to have a policy adopted before it is needed, so do not wait to put policy in place until there is a critical need for one or more types of acceleration.

One positive point about acceleration options is that generally there is no expense to implementing them. Not accelerating has a different kind of cost—a personal loss of learning time and potential. That is a loss that is difficult to recoup.

Conclusion

One characteristic of gifted children is that they learn at a faster pace than many other young people their age. Using the 18 forms of acceleration, teachers and administrators can accommodate students' needs for a faster pace in learning. The forms of acceleration must be matched to the children, selecting the type that will allow for continuous progress, beginning with the least disruptive option. All parents and educators who are considering any acceleration option should be well informed about the research on this topic. We recommend reading *A Nation Deceived: How Schools Hold Back America's Brightest Students* to gain more information and insight on acceleration.

Survival Tips

○ Start with the form of acceleration that makes the least change for the child. Check out the results and then move on to the next form of acceleration if the first one is not enough.

○ Don't hold a student back from learning experiences because others of the same age are not ready for those same experiences.

○ There are many ways to accommodate a child's need to move at a different pace in learning, and there is a strong research base for all of them. Encourage parents to learn about acceleration options if their child may benefit from one or more forms of acceleration.

Survival Toolkit

○ *The Institute for Research and Policy on Acceleration* (IRPA; http://www.accelerationinstitute.org): This organization is dedicated to the study of curricular acceleration for academically talented children. The website will provide lots of information about the procedure and policy development related to acceleration.

○ *NAGC Position Statement: Acceleration* (http://www.nagc.org/index.aspx?id=383): This is the official statement on acceleration by the National Association for Gifted Children.

○ *A Nation Deceived: How Schools Hold Back America's Brightest Students* (http://www.nationdeceived.org): Both volumes of this guide are necessary resources for anyone (parent or educator) who is considering any type of acceleration and would make a good book study for a Professional Learning Community (PLC). Start with Volume I and then proceed to Volume II, which has the research support for acceleration.

- ○ Smutny, J. F., Walker, S. Y., & Meckstroth, E. A. (2007). *Acceleration for gifted learners, K–5.* Thousand Oaks, CA: Corwin Press.

10 Making Differentiation Defensible

The "pressure for coverage" is the greatest enemy of understanding.—Howard Gardner (1993, p. 22)

Key Question

- What elements must be in place for differentiation to be defensible?

The Importance of Challenge

When should challenge first be a part of a child's learning? The answer is easy. Challenge begins at home with a child learning new things on an ongoing basis. Then, challenge must continue in school from the time the child enrolls in preschool or kindergarten. Teachers in all classes and in all grades should be committed to every child learning new things in school and making achievement gains on an ongoing basis. For the well-being of the child, the community, and the country, challenge is essential for all children. And challenge doesn't mean following the grade-level content if the child can show on a preassessment that he has met the standard. That is the signal for differentiating the curriculum.

Now here is the rub: What is challenging to one child may be too difficult or too easy for others—this is why differentiation strategies are incredibly important for all teachers to master. Teachers must remember that one doesn't start differentiating on a full-time basis when one has not been accustomed to using differentiation strategies (see Chapter 13). The key is to start with one differentiation strategy and then to build a repertoire of strategies. That takes time, but it cannot happen until you get started.

The Essentials of Differentiation

When a teacher begins to differentiate, the place to start is planning for instruction. The first question to answer is: What do you want everyone in the class to know and/or be able to do? Of course, that question leads to preassessing and raises a second question: Who already knows the information and/or can do it? It is only after the teacher plans the unit/lesson and then preassesses the skills or concepts in the unit/lesson that defensible differentiation can occur. The third question is: What do you plan for the child or children who already know or can do what is planned?

Without preassessment data, different learning experiences are just that—different. Simply offering a choice of learning experiences without matching the opportunity to learning style, readiness, or interests is different, but not differentiated in a defensible way. Information gleaned from the preassessment informs the teacher as she matches learning experiences to what the student or students already know. Preassessment is essential to ensure that each student is learning concepts and skills at an appropriately challenging level. It is not possible to learn what one already knows, and it is not appropriate to expect children to learn what is beyond their reach at that moment. Differentiation is a bit like the tale of Goldilocks and the three bears—the learning tasks can't be too difficult or too easy, but they must be just right!

Perhaps the main reason teachers do not plan for a wide range of learners is that they do not understand the need to differentiate for students who are advanced. They think gifted children will "make it on their own." The second reason, a close second, is that strategies to differentiate just have not become a natural part of their teaching routine. *Routine* is a very important word, as differentiation will only be ongoing if it fits into the way that the educator teaches on an everyday basis. The third reason for not differentiating is the emphasis schools place on proficiency. The problem with setting proficiency as a goal is that minimum competencies become maximum expectations. The cartoon in Figure 5 illustrates the problem of a child who is struggling to run but is tied to the proficiency post.

Basic strategies to differentiate instruction start with questioning strategies, writing assignments, and reading options. Recognizing that students in the class

Figure 5. Tied to the proficiency post.

are different in their levels of readiness, interests, and skills is the first step in figuring out why differentiating is essential.

PLAN

A simple formula for differentiating is PLAN—Preassessment, Learning Experiences, Assessment, and using the assessment data for planning the Next Learning Experience (see Figure 6). This approach is recommended for educators beginning to differentiate instruction.

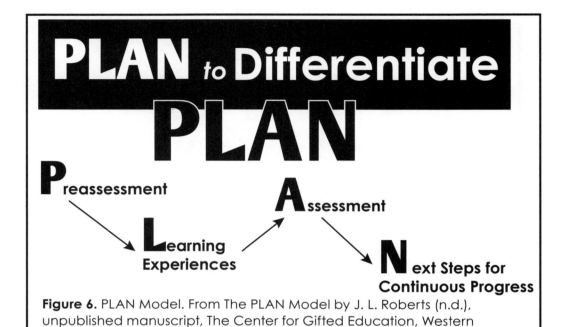

Figure 6. PLAN Model. From The PLAN Model by J. L. Roberts (n.d.), unpublished manuscript, The Center for Gifted Education, Western Kentucky University, Bowling Green, KY. Reprinted with permission.

The Principles of a Differentiated Classroom

Appropriate expectations must be in place in a classroom in order for differentiation to occur on an ongoing basis. Roberts and Inman (2009b) offered the following principles to set the stage:

- A differentiated classroom respects diversity.
- A differentiated classroom maintains high expectations.
- A differentiated classroom generates openness. (p. 20)

Data must be used to make differentiated instructional decisions. Expert Jan Lanham provides information on how to use data to make defensible decisions about differentiation.

SURVIVAL SECRETS FOR USING DATA AS THE KEY TO EFFECTIVE DIFFERENTIATION

Jan Lanham

Instructional decision making rests in the balance between the skills and concepts identified as the objectives for student learning and the instructional needs and readiness of the student. Just as we cannot teach students things they are not ready to learn, we cannot teach students things that they already know. Yet many teachers spend time trying to do just that! The use of performance data is essential to designing effective differentiation. Performance data provide a measure of student levels of mastery and will include anecdotal information, work samples, performance on teacher-made tests, any relevant assessment data, and specific preassessment data. Those data are then used to inform basic decisions about instructional groupings and pacing within a content area or unit, as well as decisions about specific instructional delivery on a weekly and daily basis.

Effective use of data is built around clear objectives that address three key questions:

1. What do I want the students to know or be able to do? *(Content and skills)*
2. What activities will be provided to explore and practice those skills? *(Guided and independent practice)*
3. What are the mastery criteria that will show that the student has achieved the objective? *(Product or performance)*

By clearly answering each of these questions in planning, differentiation becomes purposeful and matched to the needs and readiness of students. For example, a basic objective might be: *Students will demonstrate understanding of the steps in the water cycle by defining each term and placing each term correctly on a student-generated, illustrated flow chart.*

Once the objective and levels of individual accountability are identified, it is easy for the teacher to ask "Who will need extra support (and what kind of support) to successfully complete the task?" and "Who can already do this?" Data are used to answer both questions and to refine instruction to ensure continuous progress.

For those students needing extra support, definitions for the steps of the water cycle might be made available on file folder labels or as a part of a word bank, or a flow chart schematic might be provided so that students only have to provide additional details and add in the terms.

Remembering that the goal is to facilitate the students' ability to identify and use the terms, differentiation adjusts the manner in which the students practice their learning.

Based on the preassessment data, it is important to think about the students who can already do the stated task in the same way in order to ensure new learning. Typically, students would be asked to work with the skills/concepts at a more advanced level. For example, students who can already identify and sequence the scientific terms in the water cycle may be asked to use synthesis and analysis skills by illustrating and captioning the importance of each water cycle phase to the biome they have illustrated, or they may be asked to compare and contrast the phases in different seasons, or they may be asked to illustrate and explain the impact of humans on each phase of the cycle. The goal is to provide applications of the concepts at a higher level that reflects new learning for the students.

Jan W. Lanham, Ph.D.
Principal, Cox's Creek Elementary School
Nelson County Schools
Bardstown, KY

◇◇

Conclusion

Each child deserves to make continuous progress, making at least a month's achievement gain for a month in school. Differentiation makes continuous progress possible. Differentiation must accommodate the various paces of learning, interests, and academic possibilities within a group of children, even a class of gifted children.

A very effective way to begin a discussion of differentiation in a faculty meeting, a PLC, or with a parent group is to read and then discuss the book *Mrs. Spitzer's Garden*. As Mrs. Spitzer differentiates for plants in her garden, it is easy to make connections to doing so within a classroom.

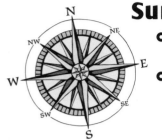

Survival Tips

- Children who learn differently must be taught differently in order to make continuous progress.

- All children need to be learning on an ongoing basis. Consequently, not all 10-year-olds are ready for the same level of math, music, writing, literature, or soccer on the same time schedule. Different learning experiences on the same concepts or skills must be matched to readiness, learning preferences, and interests if all children are to make continuous progress.

Survival Toolkit

- *Hot Topic: Differentiation of Curriculum and Instruction* (http://www.nagc.org/index2.aspx?id=978): This page of the NAGC website includes an overview of the reasons to use differentiation along with a list of links to resources on the topic.

- *Teaching Gifted Kids in Today's Regular Classroom* (http://www.nagc.org/index.aspx?id=660): This article by Susan Winebrenner discusses differentiation guidelines teachers can use in general education classrooms with their gifted students.

- Pattou, E. (2001). *Mrs. Spitzer's garden*. New York, NY: Harcourt.

- Roberts, J. L., & Inman, T. F. (2009). *Strategies for differentiating instruction: Best practices for the classroom* (2nd ed.). Waco, TX: Prufrock Press.

- Winebrenner, S. (2001). *Teaching gifted kids in the regular classroom: Strategies and techniques every teacher can use to meet the academic needs of the gifted and talented* (Rev. ed.). Minneapolis, MN: Free Spirit.

11 Preassessing in Order to Teach What Students Don't Already Know

Preassessment is the linchpin of defensible differentiation.—Roberts (2010, p. 10)

Key Question

- What preassessment tools are both easy to administer and quick to use to garner student information?

In 2000, Julian Stanley wrote an article entitled "Helping Students Learn Only What They Don't Already Know"—a title alone that tells us why preassessment is the natural and necessary step that follows planning a unit (you can't preassess until you have planned what the students are to know and to be able to do). After all, if the student already knows or can do what you want the unit to accomplish, it presents a wonderful opportunity to allow him to learn about the same topic but at a more complex and in-depth level. Do you remember all of the times you have said, "I wish I had more time to teach . . . "? Preassessment allows you to find that desired time for one student, a few students, or all students. Of course, preassessment guides your decision about matching learning experiences to the interests, needs, and readiness of the learners.

Just think of what your perception would be if you went to see your physician, and she prescribed the same drugs to you that all patients got that particular day—after all, it was Tuesday, and that was what was planned for Tuesday. Of course, that makes no sense at all, yet the one-lesson-fits-all-students approach to teaching follows the same logic. It doesn't work for all of the patients, and it doesn't work for all of the students. In fact, Reis and colleagues (1993) found that gifted elementary children knew more than half of the content when they started the year, leading the subtitle of their study on content to be *Why Not Let High Ability Students Start School in January?*

Preassessment information, including interest and learning preference inventories, proves to be important for knowing which questions, writing assignments, and reading options will allow each student to make continuous progress.

Types of Preassessment

There are many ways to preassess what students know before teaching a unit. To do this routinely, the preassessment must be easy to use. That is, it must be easy in terms of creating the preassessment and tabulating the results. Here are examples of ways to try to gather information about what your students already know and are able to do.

The T-W-H Chart

Let's start with a familiar way to preassess—the K-W-L Chart, but in this case it is called the T-W-H Chart (see Figure 7). The T column lets the student tell you what he thinks about the topic (not quite so specific as knowing about a topic). The W column allows him to tell you what he wants to know about the topic, and the H column provides the opportunity for the student to let you know how he would like to learn about the topic.

The T-W-H Chart garners a lot of information about each student's knowledge on the topic of study, as well as what about the topic interests him and how he would like to learn about the topic. Can you use all of the students' suggestions? Of course not. However, when you can use a suggestion about instruction from a reluctant learner, you have made an important connection that can motivate the child. Information you learn from the completed T-W-H charts can help you group children of like interests and similar levels of readiness. The charts can be sorted easily into three piles—those who know quite a bit about the topic, those who know a little, and those who are new to the topic. If you find out that none of the students are familiar with the topic, it is fair game to plan the same learning experiences for all children. You may find out that all or most students know a lot about the subject. However, it is far more likely that some students will have interests in the topic that vary from "very interested" to "unaware."

T - W - H CHART

Topic/Unit_____   **Name**_____

What do you Think about this topic?	**What do you Want to learn about this topic?**	**How do you want to learn about this topic?**

Figure 7. T-W-H Chart. Adapted from *Strategies for Differentiating Instruction: Best Practices for the Classroom*, 2nd ed., p. 50, by J. L. Roberts and T. F. Inman, 2009, Waco, TX: Prufrock Press. Revised with permission.

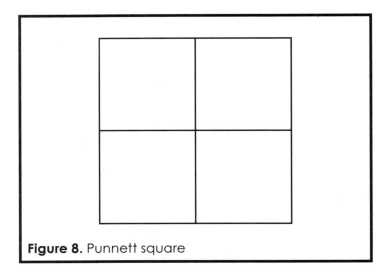

Figure 8. Punnett square

Open-Ended Writing

Another easy way to preassess is to give the class 5 minutes to write about the topic they are to study. Open-ended writing can reveal a lot about what each student knows or does not know about the topic. A quick read of their responses tells you what each student brings to the new unit of study.

End-of-the-Unit Assessment or End-of-the-Previous-Unit Assessment

Using assessments given at the conclusion of the unit or at the end of the previous unit can be informative as preassessments. The assessment given at the end of the previous unit works well as a preassessment (and takes no extra time) if the material to be learned is sequential.

Punnett Square

The punnett square provides a quick way to see what the students in your class already know about a concept. In one quadrant the student provides his understanding of the definition of the concept, in another he writes an example of the concept, and in another he gives a nonexample of the concept. The fourth quadrant is where he provides any other information on the concept.

Preassessing for Learning Styles

Preassessments can also be used to determine the learners' preferred ways of learning or their interests concerning a topic to be studied. The preassessment

The Great Depression Preassessment

Circle all that apply.
- I have heard of the Great Depression.
- I have read some about the Great Depression.
- I have talked with relatives about the Great Depression.
- I have not yet been interested in the Great Depression.

Circle the response that best describes your experience interviewing people to get information.
- I enjoy interviewing to learn.
- I have no experience interviewing for a project but think I would like to give it a try.
- I have interviewed for a project but would prefer getting information another way.

Circle the aspect of the Great Depression that most interests you.
- Life in your town during the Great Depression.
- The life of a hobo during the Great Depression.
- The stock market crash of 1929.
- Other? You suggest a topic related to the Great Depression in the United States.

Circle the final product that you would prefer to complete to showcase what you have learned.
- A radio show
- A series of illustrations or graphs to accompany a report
- A monologue
- Other? Specify.

Figure 9. The Great Depression preassessment. From "Preassessment: The Linchpin for Defensible Differentiation," by J. L. Roberts, 2010, *The Challenge, 24,* p. 10. Copyright 2010 Center for Gifted Studies, Western Kentucky University. Reprinted with permission.

on the Great Depression (Roberts, 2010, p. 10) shown in Figure 9 is an example of this type of preassessment.

Stoplight Questions

You can give young students the opportunity to color-code their answers using the colors found in a traffic light. Green means he definitely knows it, yellow says that he thinks it is correct but guessed, and red tells you that he has no idea. This coloring system works with young students and can be used with older ones as well.

Five Most Difficult Questions

If you provide the students with the opportunity to answer the five most difficult questions in the unit and the student(s) can answer them with at least 80% accuracy, you have strong evidence that the student doesn't need to study the unit in the same way as students who don't have that level of understanding of the content or the demonstration of skills.

Words From Students

Sometimes you can glean important information about what the child knows about a topic from her conversation. A new first grader who tells her teacher, "I really don't want to hurt your feelings, but we are doing kindergarten work" and a boy in kindergarten who correctly explains negative numbers are providing information about what they already know and can do. A middle school student who is discussing a book that the English teacher is surprised that anyone has read can alert the teacher that the child has advanced literacy skills. Clues appear all of the time, but you must be paying attention to what you hear from young people or observe them doing in order for this informal information to be useful and inform instructional decisions.

Jan Lanham describes important points that increase the effectiveness of preassessment.

◇◇◇

SURVIVAL SECRETS FOR PRETESTING

Jan Lanham

The use of student performance data is a foundation for appropriate instructional planning and differentiation for all students. Although it is only one type of performance data, a cornerstone of that data is the topic or unit pretest commonly administered to group students for instruction within the unit. After watching the administration of pretests across countless classrooms, some important practices to ensure effectiveness emerge:

1. *Identify unit/lesson skills and concepts.* Identify specific skills and concepts for the unit and design a pretest that looks similar to the posttest to identify student levels of awareness and mastery relative to those target skills and concepts. Select pretest items that will inform instruction (e.g.,

If students miss this question, what instruction is needed to make sure they can answer other questions like this?).

2. *Preteach.* It is important to spend some time "priming the pump" to ensure that the pretest data are accurate. For many content-related vocabulary terms and concepts, students may not have used those terms or procedures since the same unit last year, but they did master it when it was taught, so they do not need to go back to the very beginning. Spending a class period or two preteaching the skills, vocabulary, and concepts in the unit proves valuable to generating the most accurate data for grouping students relative to their content readiness. For students who need multiple repetitions, preteaching is one more repetition. For students who were just "rusty," preteaching refreshes their memories and allows them to more accurately show what they know.

3. *Minimize the pretest threat.* Help students understand that the pretest is a strategy to validate what students know. Projecting a message that student time is valued is often a powerful motivator. Make sure students know that the pretest is not related to a grade, but is a single piece of information to help inform instruction. Pretest data can be used as pre-post comparisons to help students see how much they have improved, but they should not ever be used to negatively impact grades.

4. *Use the data for instructional groupings and differentiation.* Analysis of pretest data should be conducted in order to identify students with common instructional needs, to identify unit concepts that are already mastered by most of the group, and to create purposeful targeted groupings that provide for appropriate access to the level and pace of instruction needed for each student. The data can then be used to adjust the depth and complexity of instruction, of activities, and of student products based on that data analysis.

Pretesting is one of the most important tools for diagnostic differentiation of instruction.

Jan W. Lanham, Ph.D.
Principal, Cox's Creek Elementary School
Nelson County Schools
Bardstown, KY

Conclusion

One further recommendation about preassessment is that you keep the students' individual preassessments. They give you a way to talk with the students about their growth in learning over time. They also let you show parents why their children are doing specific assignments, so you can discuss the match between the assignments and the interests, needs, and readiness of the child. Overall, preassessment is a valuable tool in planning and differentiating instruction for gifted learners.

Survival Tips

○ Learn as much as you can about your students. It will make your students feel valued, and it will help you match instruction to the student to enhance learning.

○ The preassessment sets the starting point, but the outstanding teacher establishes the final destination.

○ The teacher needs to inform parents that the purpose of preassessment is to see what the child already knows so time isn't wasted teaching those concepts and/or skills. Teachers need to know that students are not expected to answer all of the questions correctly on a preassessment; rather, it is a way to plan learning experiences that will match the student's readiness to learn certain skills and about particular topics. Otherwise, parents may be anxious when they hear that their children had an assessment (test) and that they didn't know the answers to most of the questions that were asked.

Survival Toolkit

○ *Byrdseed Gifted: Differentiating Within a Gifted Classroom* (http://www.byrdseed.com/differentiating-within-a-gifted-classroom): This blog entry shares one teacher's use of pretests to create groups in his class and provides a helpful explanation of how preassessment can be used in the classroom.

○ *Differentiation Tips for Teachers: Practical Strategies for the Classroom: Part I: Preassessment* (http://www.nagc.org/uploadedFiles/Articles/Differentiation_Pt1-ChallengeWinter05.pdf):

This article overviews the need for teachers to employ preassessment as a differentiation tool in their classrooms.

○ *Preassessment* (http://daretodifferentiate.wikispaces.com/Pre-Assessment): This wiki provides links to a variety of preassessment tools and articles on the topic.

12 Strategies to Light the Fire of Learning

Education is not the filling of a pail, but the lighting of a fire.—William Butler Yeats

Key Question

- When many teachers first heard about 21st-century skills, that century had not arrived; however, we now live in the second decade of that new century. Now you need to prepare students for tomorrow's world. What do students need to know and be able to do to be successful in the 21st century?

The Higher Education Opportunity Act and Gifted Learners

The Higher Education Opportunity Act (2008) included specific language about gifted children and the need to tailor instruction to address their needs. Gifted children were included in the Higher Education Opportunity Act (HEOA) for the first time in 2008. Specifically, the HEOA included the following language:

(23) TEACHING SKILLS—The term "teaching skills" means skills that enable a teacher to—

    A: increase student learning, achievement, and the ability to apply knowledge;

    B: effectively convey and explain academic subject matter;

    C: effectively teach higher-order analytical, evaluation, problem-solving, and communication skills;

    D: employ strategies grounded in the disciplines or teaching and learning that—

        a. are based on empirically-based practice and scientifically valid research, where applicable, related to teaching and learning;

        b. are specific to academic subject matter; and

        c. focus on the identification of students' specific learning needs, particularly students with disabilities, students who are limited English proficient, **students who are gifted and talented**, and students with low literacy levels, and the tailoring of academic instruction to such needs. (3132–3133; emphasis added)

The inclusion of gifted children in the Higher Education Opportunity Act is worth noting and sharing as you advocate and plan instruction for gifted and talented students.

A single chapter cannot begin to be comprehensive of the many strategies available for teaching gifted kids. Consequently, a few important strategies are highlighted—ones to engage students in learning and hopefully light the fire of their lifelong learning.

Continuous Learning Opportunities

Allow students to learn on an ongoing basis. If every child in the class is capable of doing the activity, they should all have the opportunity to do so. If everyone isn't ready for that learning experience, children who are ready should be given the opportunity. This is where differentiation becomes so important for children (see Chapter 13).

Encourage Higher Level Thinking

Require thinking at high levels. Twenty-first century skills require thinking, just as gifted education has for several decades. Critical and creative thinking are very important skills that should be required and developed in all classes, no matter the content. Problem-based learning (PBL) focuses on a discrepant situation or problem. Then the students use their thinking and collaboration skills to provide solutions to the problem. Remember that the world's biggest problems have no magic bullet solutions, so students need strategies to solve problems and experience doing so.

Choose strategies that encourage higher level thinking in your classes. Remember that if you or the students can find the answer using a simple Internet search, then it isn't a higher level question. Here are some tips for making sure the questions you ask are at a higher level:

- Ask who, what, when, and where questions, but then move on to questions that ask students to combine ideas in new ways.
- Ask if-then questions—questions that require speculating as to what could happen.
- Carry a card with the higher level questions you have planned. Planning questions in advance will spark your thinking, especially if you are used to asking lower level questions.

Engage the Students

Select strategies that actively engage students in the learning experiences. Engagement may relate to the topic, the skills required to learn at high levels, and/or the product. When young people are engaged in learning, it is hard to separate work from play. Engagement usually is the result of hands-on, minds-on learning experiences. Just hands-on activities are not enough, as real learning experiences must also be minds-on.

Also make sure to provide resources that engage students in learning. Advanced readers need resources at their challenge levels—neither too easy nor too difficult. de Wet, Gubbins, and Vahindi (2005) described the Schoolwide Enrichment Model in Reading (SEM-R) and offered strategies for engaging advanced readers using appropriately challenging, rather than grade-level, reading materials. Downloadable materials are available at the National Research Center on the Gifted and Talented website (http://www.gifted.uconn.edu/nrcgt.html) that provide questions on characters, nonfiction, biography, reading attitudes, and other literary topics. These questions can stimulate discussions on any high-interest books you select for your classroom.

You can also use data to engage students in learning. Renzulli, Heilbronner, and Siegle (2010) described strategies to get students involved in hands-on investigations using data-gathering skills (see Table 2 for a suggestion of instruments teachers can use in their classrooms). Their book, *Think Data: Getting Kids Involved in Hands-On Investigations With Data-Gathering Instruments*, is a good resource for teachers interested in using data collection to engage students in learning.

Table 2
Instruments for Data Collection

Name of Instrument	What It Measures
Digital sound level meter	Sound wave amplitude in decibels
Protractor	Angles
Caliper	Distance between opposite sides
Kitchen scale	Mass in grams
Walking tape measurer	Distance traveled by a wheel
Clap-o-meter	Volume of applause
Odometer	Distance
Glo-germ kit	"Germ" residue
Salt check monitor	Salt level in substance
pH meter or pH level indicator strips	pH levels (1–14) of a substance
Tally counter	Counting units
Digital thermometer	Temperature
Instant ocean hydrometer	Specific gravity (density) of water
Barometer	Air pressure
Soil meter	Soil pH
Blood pressure monitor	Systolic and diastolic blood pressure
Stopwatch, egg timer, sundial	Time
Planimeter	Area
Accelerometer	Acceleration
Pedometer	Number of steps
Speedometer	Speed, velocity
Wattmeter	Electrical power

Adapted from *Think Data: Getting Kids Involved in Hands-on Investigations With Data-Gathering Instruments,* by J. S. Renzulli, N. N. Heilbronner, and D. Siegle, 2010, Mansfield Center, CT: Creative Learning Press. Copyright 2010 Creative Learning Press. Reprinted with permission.

Teachers can offer technology to engage learners, particularly reluctant learners who are eager to use the classroom technology tools but dread written or paper-based assignments. One way to do this is to offer students a choice of products to demonstrate what has been learned. Technology can be used in many ways, one of which is to engage students in projects based on their interest in the technology involved in creating the product; some students may have little interest in a topic, but if technology is involved in the learning, they become engaged. For example, creating a podcast or developing a blog may catch the interest of students who are weary of writing another report about what they have learned on a topic.

Provide Problem-Based Learning Experiences

Create situations for students to become scientists, mathematicians, archeologists, and other professionals. When your students don the lab coat and engage in the thinking process that a scientist uses, learning is more engaging than when reading a science text and discussing the topic in the chapter. The Center for Gifted Education at the College of William and Mary (see http://www. cfge.wm.edu) has developed science units to engage children in the act of being young scientists. Each unit requires students to develop their own answers and thoughts about a real-life problem. The units can be purchased from Prufrock Press (http://www.prufrock.com). At the University of Connecticut, a federally funded project called Project M³ has developed mathematics materials that lead students to think like mathematicians (see http://www.gifted.uconn.edu/ projectm3/about.htm). The units developed by this project can be found at http:// www.gifted.uconn.edu/projectm3/teachers_curriculum.htm. Such thinking has positive implications for creating lifelong learners.

Provide Mentors

Real-life experiences also include various types of mentoring. The first level is shadowing. A student spends a day with a veterinarian to check out what a day in the career of a vet is like, or goes to the state capitol to follow a senator to learn about the business of creating legislation. Mentoring that is a long-term relationship focuses on an interest shared by the mentor and mentee. Often that interest is a research area the student wishes to pursue. Successful mentorships depend on mutual benefits for both partners.

Implement Project-Based Learning

Involve students in project-based learning. Project-based learning provides a great way to engage students in high-level learning, and this type of application of knowledge is in tune with 21st-century learning goals. Students often put forth their best effort when working on a project, especially when they have an element of choice in the project. Perhaps a student gets to pose the specific question to be addressed about a topic the class is studying. Perhaps she has the choice of which product she'll create to communicate what she discovered as she learned about the specific topic. Either way, choice is often a motivator for young people in a classroom.

Conclusion

Make sure you are providing assignments or learning tasks that are worthy of the students' time and energy. Busy work is never a winner in the eyes of students, and such assignments waste the teacher's valuable teaching time as well. Differentiate assignments to ensure that students aren't running in place but are learning on an ongoing basis.

Survival Tips

- Make sure you provide minds-on learning experiences. If they are hands-on, too, that is great, but they must be minds-on.

- Parents need to know about strategies that will allow their children to be the most advanced learners they can be.

Survival Toolkit

- *Curriculum Units* (http://www.gifted.uconn.edu/projectm3/teachers_curriculum.htm): This link takes teachers to the curriculum units developed by Project M³ at the University of Connecticut.

- *Gifted Child Today* (GCT; http://journals.prufrock.com/IJP/b/gifted-child-today): GCT is filled with practical strategies for teachers. It also reviews new products for teachers of gifted students.

- *William and Mary Curriculum* (http://www.cfge.wm.edu/curriculum.htm): This site provides an overview of the various curriculum units (including *Budding Botanists*, listed below) that can be purchased from Prufrock Press (http://www.prufrock.com).

- Center for Gifted Education. (2010). *Budding botanists*. Waco, TX: Prufrock Press.

- Karnes, F. A., & Bean, S. M. (2007). *Methods and materials for teaching the gifted* (3rd ed.). Waco, TX: Prufrock Press.

- Robinson, A., Shore, B. A., & Enersen, D. L. (2007). *Best practices in gifted education: An evidence-based guide*. Waco, TX: Prufrock Press.

13 Strategies to Differentiate Instruction

In the United States, differentiation was a way of life in the one-room schoolhouse. There, the teacher knew students would vary greatly in age, experience, motivation to learn, and proficiency. To effectively instruct the range of students, teachers had to be flexible in their use of time, space, materials, student groupings, and instructional contact with learners.—Carol Tomlinson (2005, p. 8)

Key Question

- What are all of the things you can do to see that all students understand increasingly complex concepts, engage in learning that challenges, and develop a work ethic—important ingredients for successful learners?

That one-size-fits-all lessons do not allow for all students to make continuous progress is clear. Teachers must modify their strategies for children who need more time and more basic explanations to grasp the concept. Likewise, children who learn at a faster pace and already understand the concept being taught need modifications in order to continue to learn and not just mark time. Remember the drawing of a learner tied to the proficiency post on p. 83? This chapter will provide examples of various ways to modify the curriculum to provide challenging learning opportunities for all young people. Of course,

---

The Six Categories of the Cognitive Process Dimension

1. REMEMBER—Retrieve relevant knowledge from long-term memory

2. UNDERSTAND—Construct meaning from instructional messages, including oral, written, and graphic communication

3. APPLY—Carry out or use a procedure in a given situation

4. ANALYZE—Break material into constituent parts and determine how parts relate to one another and to an overall structure or purpose

5. EVALUATE—Make judgments based on criteria and standards

6. CREATE—Put elements together to form a coherent or functional whole, reorganize elements into a new pattern or structure

Figure 10. The six categories of the Cognitive Process Dimension. From *Strategies for Differentiating Instruction: Best Practices for the Classroom* (2nd ed.), by J. L. Roberts and T. F. Inman, 2009, p. 66, Waco, TX: Prufrock Press. Copyright 2009 Prufrock Press. Reprinted with permission.

---

the starting point is the preassessment of what the students know and are able to do in relation to the topic of the unit and skills to be developed. Information gained from inventories of learning styles, preferences, and interests will also help you tailor differentiated learning experiences to make them motivating and appropriately challenging to the students in your class.

The Revised Cognitive Taxonomy

The revised Taxonomy of Cognitive Objectives (Anderson et al., 2001) provides a means of differentiating the level of thinking in learning experiences. Figure 10 describes the six categories in the revised taxonomy.

Differentiating learning experiences using this model means keeping the content/concept the same for all six cognitive levels but varying the process (the verb) and offering a choice of product when possible. An example of a planning chart for differentiating learning experiences with the revised taxonomy follows in Figure 11.

	PROCESS	CONTENT	PRODUCT
CREATE	Create	Fractions	Open Product/ Your Choice
	Create examples of an interesting, unusual way to use fractions or to teach someone else about fractions. Select the product to present your ideas.		
EVALUATE	Justify	Fractions	Persuasive Essay or Debate
	Justify learning about fractions in a persuasive essay or debate.		
ANALYZE	Compare	Fractions	Venn Diagram or Poster
	Compare fractions and decimals on a Venn diagram or poster.		
APPLY	Organize	Fractions	Number Line
	Organize fractions on a number line.		
UNDERSTAND	Explain	Fractions	Discussion or Role Play
	Explain fractions in a discussion or a role play.		
REMEMBER	Identify	Fractions	Chart or Pictures
	Identify fractions on a chart or with pictures.		

Figure 11. Bloom chart for fractions. From *Strategies for Differentiating Instruction: Best Practices for the Classroom* (2nd ed.), by J. L. Roberts and T. F. Inman, 2009, p. 72, Waco, TX: Prufrock Press. Copyright 2009 Prufrock Press. Reprinted with permission.

Not all students will do all six of the learning experiences, but the preassessment will guide each student to choose two of the three learning options that will require him to think in order to complete the tasks. Otherwise, some advanced students will choose the easier options in order to speed through the assignment.

One caution for the teacher in planning learning experiences at the create level: Designing a poem or a poster about the concept does not qualify the learning activity for the top level (creating). Instead the student must be required to think creatively about the content or concept that was the reason for designing this set of differentiated learning experiences. In this example, students had to think creatively about fractions.

Venn Diagrams

All teachers use Venn diagrams, but not all use the Venn diagram to differentiate learning experiences for their students. Kanevsky (2003) described this strategy, and Roberts and Inman (2009b) developed examples for using Venn diagrams. Very simply, differentiating using the Venn diagram allows the teacher to match the challenge of a learning experience to the students' levels of readiness based on preassessment results. All students are engaged in the same task, whether it is examining characters in a short story or novel, different colonies in U.S. history, or types of severe weather. The difference is that some students will be doing that task with one, two, three, or even four characters or colonies. The templates that Roberts and Inman provided are ovals rather than circles, as they provide more space on which the student can write.

Figure 12 shows an example of a differentiated learning experience using the Venn diagram. All students list adjectives to describe one or more characters in the book. Some will work with one character while others will compare and contrast two characters. Still others will work with three characters, and a small number may be ready to look at four characters in relation to each other. The key to successful differentiation is to match the level of challenge to the readiness of the student to complete the learning experience. Once again, preassessment data provide the rationale for the match between the learning experience and the student.

Think-Tac-Toe Model

Another way to differentiate learning experiences to provide challenge and interest for students is the think-tac-toe model. Students do not try to do learning experiences to get an X on the think-tac-toe board but rather to complete ones that allow them to demonstrate what they have learned in a unit of study.

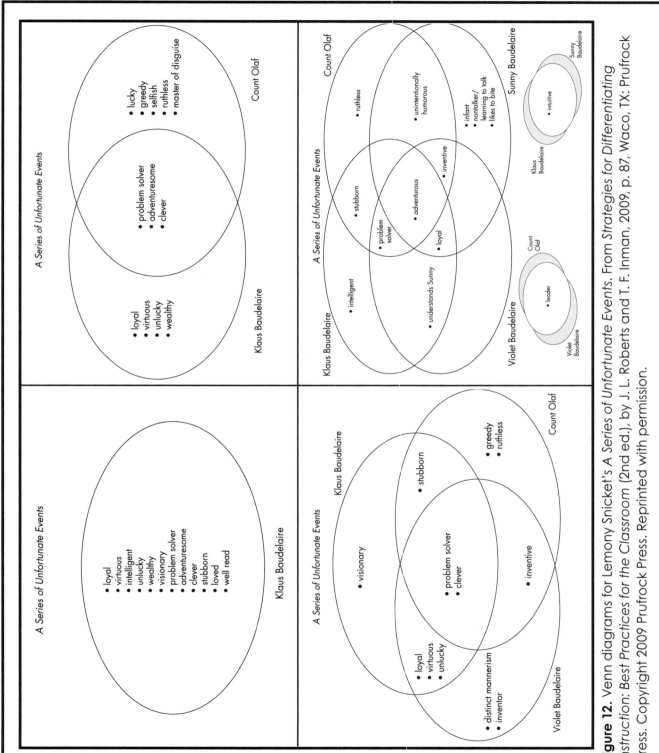

Figure 12. Venn diagrams for Lemony Snicket's *A Series of Unfortunate Events*. From *Strategies for Differentiating Instruction: Best Practices for the Classroom* (2nd ed.), by J. L. Roberts and T. F. Inman, 2009, p. 87, Waco, TX: Prufrock Press. Copyright 2009 Prufrock Press. Reprinted with permission.

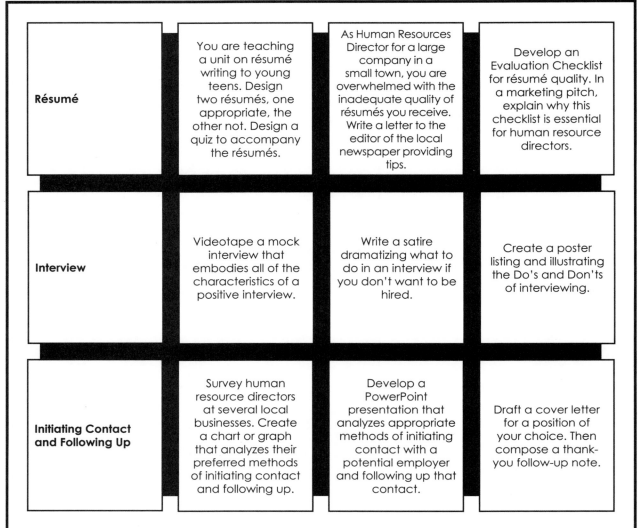

Figure 13. Think-tac-toe: Careers—Getting the job done. From *Strategies for Differentiating Instruction: Best Practices for the Classroom* (2nd ed.), by J. L. Roberts and T. F. Inman, 2009, p. 110, Waco, TX: Prufrock Press. Copyright 2009 Prufrock Press. Reprinted with permission.

Usually the students are asked to complete a learning experience on various levels, highlighting the important concepts that are being studied in a unit.

An example of a think-tac-toe is found in Figure 13. Students choose one learning experience to complete on each row, which ensures that they have learned important concepts during the course of the unit study. The think-tac-toe allows students an element of choice as they demonstrate what they have learned using a variety of products.

Another level of differentiation with the think-tac-toe model of differentiation is to have two different think-tac-toes, with one more challenging than the other. The two think-tac-toes look very similar, but the teacher ensures that each student has choices on the think-tac-toe that will make sure he works at an appropriate level of challenge. A tremendous advantage of this level of differentiation, as well as with using one basic think-tac-toe, is that all students can discuss what they have learned together because all are focusing on the same concepts as they complete different products.

Tiered Lessons

Tiering lessons means that all students are studying the same subject; however, they are all doing so at a level that challenges them academically. Adams and Pierce (2006) offered examples of tiered lessons. Lessons may be tiered based on readiness, interests, or learning preferences. An example of a tiered lesson is shown in Figure 14.

Another example of a tiered lesson focuses on the concepts of force and motion. After all students go to the lab and conduct experiments on force and motion, the teacher passes out follow-up assignments. The determining factor in which students get which assignments is information the teacher has about how the students prefer to learn and their strengths. The assignments are to write a description of a car coming down a mountain road using the concepts of force and motion, to design an experiment using these concepts, or to describe three to five examples in everyday life that utilize the concepts of force and motion at work.

Choice of Products

Often a student having a choice of product to demonstrate what she has learned results in the student doing her best work. After all, she is motivated to do so, as she has likely selected a product that interests her and that relies on her strengths. A list of products (see Table 3) can be lengthy. Categorizing the products will let the teacher offer choices of products to students. Roberts and Inman (2009a) categorized products into the following five categories: kinesthetic, oral, technological, visual, and written.

Although students should not always have product options that match their learning style or preferences, occasionally each student should have the opportunity to do so. Sometimes the teacher will not care how the students show what they have learned, and then it is appropriate to offer a choice of products. For example, students may be able to show what they learned about the Civil War in a monologue that is written and performed, a PowerPoint with a presentation, or a series of illustrations. The key is to provide choices that will appeal to students with different learning preferences and interests and not to offer three different written products.

Sample Tiered Lesson 4
Needs of Plants: Grade 2

Subject: Science

Grade: Second

Standard: Content Standard C: All students should develop understanding of the characteristics of organisms.

Key Concept: Organisms have basic needs and can survive only in environments in which their needs can be met.

Essential Understanding: Plants need soil, sunlight, and water in order to grow.

Background: The students have already studied the needs of animals as part of their work with living things. The activity introduces a lesson that allows students to discover what is necessary for plants to grow. Students will use guided discovery to learn the needs of plants. Students who need step-by-step directions and more structure should work in Tier I. Tier II is less structured, and Tier III is the least structured.

All groups will be investigating the needs of plants. Available materials should include soil, water, cups, milk cartons or pots, seeds (some seeds that work well are radish, beans, or the Wisconsin FastPlants available from Carolina Biological Supply), metric ruler, metric measuring cup, and markers.

Tier I:
These students will be given step-by-step directions to perform an investigation that will assist them in determining what plants need in order to grow. Students will use the variables of soil, water, and sunlight to determine what plants need to live. Most science books will have a detailed step-by-step experiment with plants that can be used or you may choose to write out the directions.

Tier II:
These students will investigate the needs of plants by varying the amount of water given to the plants while keeping the amount of soil and sunlight constant. Provide directions for the students to begin the investigation (materials, how to plant, amount of soil to use, number of seeds per cup, etc.), but have them determine the number of cups they will use and how to vary the water in each cup.

Tier III:
These students will read The Empty Pot by Demi (1996) or another story that deals with the needs of plants. Students will design and carry out an investigation based on the story. Students should include their research question, hypothesis, materials, procedure, data collection, results, and conclusion. As students carry out their investigation, provide assistance as needed.

Assessment: The teacher will use a flip card chart to assess students' progress during the design and implementation of the investigations for formative assessment. Science journals and activity sheets that include the information necessary to replicate the investigation, as well as the data tables and conclusions serve as summative assessment. Appropriate results (e.g., plants grew, plants didn't grow) based on experimental conditions also serve as summative evaluation.

Figure 14. Sample tiered lesson. From *Differentiating Instruction: A Practical Guide to Tiered Lessons in the Elementary Grades*, by C. M. Adams and R. L. Pierce, 2006, pp. 51–52, Waco, TX: Prufrock Press. Copyright 2006 Prufrock Press. Reprinted with permission.

Table 3
Possible Products

Advertisement (print)
Advertisement (radio)
Advertisement (television)
Application
Article
Audiotape
Biography
Blog
Blueprint
Book
Book Cover
Brochure
Bulletin Board
Cartoon
Case Study
Chart
Choral Reading
Collage
Collection
Column
Commercial
Computer Graphic
Computer Program
Costume
Creative Writing
Dance
Debate
Demonstration
Diagram
Dialogue
Diary
Diorama
Display
Document-Based Question
Documentary
Dramatic Presentation
Drawing
Editorial
Essay
Exhibit/Display
Experiment
Evaluation Form

Feature Article
Film
Game
Graph
Graphic Organizer
Greeting Card
Illustrated Story
Illustration
Interview (live)
Interview (recorded)
Interview (written)
Invention
Journal
Lesson
Letter (business)
Letter (friendly)
Letter to Editor
Mask
Matrix
Mathematical Formula
Mentorship
Mime
Mock Court
Mock Trial (attorney)
Mock Trial (defendant)
Mock Trial (judge)
Mock Trial (plaintiff)
Model
Monologue
Movie
Mural
Museum
Museum Exhibit
Musical
Newscast
Newsletter
Newspaper Story
Open Response
Oral History
Oral Report
Outline
Painting
Peer Evaluation
Pamphlet

Photo
Photo Essay
Picture
Plan
Play
Podcast
Poem
Political Cartoon
Poster
PowerPoint
Presentation
Project
Public Service Announcement (radio)
Public Service Announcement (television)
Puppet
Puppet Show
Questionnaire
Research Report
Review
Science Fair Project
Sculpture
Scrapbook
Script
Service Learning Project
Simulation
Skit
Song
Speech (oral)
Speech (written)
Story
Story Telling
Survey
Technical Report
Technical Writing
Timeline
Transparency
Venn Diagram
Video
Video Game
Volunteer Activity
Webpage
Wiki
Written Report

Products List

Dr. Julia Roberts and Ms. Tracy Inman,
The Center for Gifted Studies,
Western Kentucky University
gifted@wku.edu

It is very important that you provide guidance on how to complete the product so that it is of high quality. A rubric can provide the standards that need to be addressed with each product. Another way to guide the development of products is using the DAP Tool (the Developing and Assessing Products Tool; Roberts and Inman, 2009a). The advantage the DAP Tool offers is that you can provide a choice of products without needing to write new rubrics, as the DAP Tool is a protocol to be used with products again and again. In a nutshell, the DAP Tool is:

1. consistent in its components (content, presentation, creativity, and reflection);
2. ready for differentiation, as each DAP Tool has three tiers that provide varying levels of difficulty; and
3. of high level in that the scoring goes two levels above proficient with the highest one being a professional level, one that few students will be expected to reach.

Differentiation with products allows teachers to offer students opportunities to learn as they engage in developing products that have some choice and often may be in their preferred way of learning. Of course, sometimes students will need to complete products for other reasons. For example, all students may be expected to write a research paper or to conduct an experiment for a science fair.

Grouping for Instructional Purposes

Grouping for instructional purposes can be done in many ways, with the goal always being to allow students to make continuous progress; therefore, grouping options must be linked with differentiation strategies. Some types of grouping are the result of acceleration and were discussed in Chapter 9. However, it is difficult to have a discussion of differentiation without looking at various grouping possibilities. Karen Rogers presents different grouping options with a chart describing each (see Table 4).

◇◇◇

SURVIVAL SECRETS FOR GROUPING GIFTED CHILDREN FOR LEARNING AND SOCIALIZATION

Karen B. Rogers

Grouping has suffered a long uphill battle with people in general education, not because it is damaging for gifted learners, but more because the benefits it provides gifted learners cannot be matched when it is used with other groups of differing ability levels. An estimated 15 research syntheses about the academic, social, and psychological (e.g., self-esteem, attitude toward subject) effects of grouping have been conducted since the early 1980s, not to say that the issue was not claimed and disclaimed before that time. So what does this research say? Basically, the opponents are correct about its effects on learners not identified as gifted: There seems to be little academic benefit for them (Slavin, 1987, 1990). Recent research, however, has found that for these learners there are some self-efficacy and socialization benefits to be gained when they are placed with others who are of equal ability or who are capable of performing at their respective levels (Rogers, 2007). But the academic, social, and psychological effects for learners with gifts and talents are substantial: We can expect, on average, about an *additional* half year's academic jump (beyond the one year the children make by just being in school) when compared to equally capable learners who have been placed in mixed-ability classes or mixed-ability learning groups (Rogers, 2007). Socialization is also improved, not so much in terms of the social skills they exhibit, but in terms of their ability to work *with* others like themselves and *learn from* these intellectual or academic peers (Rogers, 2007). Attitudes toward what they are learning also improve remarkably (Kulik & Kulik, 1991). Self-efficacy remains fairly constant: If these learners felt good about what they were capable of doing before they were grouped, it remains so, as does the converse.

In looking more closely at the strategy of grouping, there are basically two forms of placing children together: (1) *ability grouping*, for which learners of the same intellectual or ability level are placed together for their learning; and (2) *performance grouping*, for which learners are placed with others performing at the same high level (usually beyond grade level). The forms of ability grouping in general show 1 ½ years of academic gains in all or most subject areas when these gifted learners are placed in full-time gifted programs, gifted magnet schools, a gifted school-within-a-school, cluster-grouped classrooms, or like-ability cooperative groups within a classroom. The forms of performance grouping generally show approximately three-fifths to four-fifths of an additional year's academic gain when these high-performing learners are placed in regrouped classes that "start" at their current performance level, performance cluster grouping, within-class grouping, like-performance cooperative groups, or cross-graded classes.

Table 4
Glossary of Grouping Option Terms

Ability-Grouped Options	Any strategy that identifies and sorts students into learning groups by their ability level (usually involving a test of ability or IQ as the measure used).
• Gifted magnet school; governor's school	High-ability students attend a specialized school for all academic learning at differentiated, accelerated level.
• Full-time gifted program; school-within-a school program	High-ability students attend a special school either as a separate school or a specialized school within a neighborhood school for all academic learning at differentiated, accelerated level.
• Cluster grouping	The top five to eight high-ability students at each grade level are "clustered" within an otherwise heterogeneous class so that the teacher can differentiate for this group for a proportionate amount of classroom time in all academic subjects.
• Like-ability cooperative learning groups	Each teacher creates high-ability cooperative group (top three to four students in a classroom) and differentiates the learning task and expectations for this group in a specific academic subject area.
Performance-Grouped Options	**Any strategy that identifies and sorts students into learning groups by their current performance/achievement levels (usually involving standardized or curriculum-based measure of performance).**
• Regrouping for specific instruction	The highest performing students at a grade level are placed in a separate class for their instruction, with concomitant curriculum at their current performance levels, regardless of actual grade placement; can be done at all building levels.
• Honors or advanced classes (could also include Advanced Placement and International Baccalaureate programs)	The highest performing students are placed in separate classes for their instruction, with concomitant curriculum beyond what is offered as "regular" curriculum outcomes; usually found at middle and high school levels.

Table 4, continued

• Performance cluster grouping	The top five to eight high-performing students in a specific subject, such as reading or mathematics, are "clustered" with one otherwise heterogeneous class so that the teacher can differentiate in that academic area. At the elementary level, this usually means two cluster classrooms—one for reading/language arts and one for mathematics. Students who are in the top performance groups of each area can usually take part in both classrooms when the two teachers coordinate their differentiation schedules.
• Within-class grouping	Each teacher sorts students by their readiness (and perhaps interest) for each unit within an academic area, such that there might be three groups being differentiated accordingly in reading units, social studies, science, and math. This is sometimes referred to as *flexible grouping*.
• Performance cooperative learning groups	Each teacher creates a high-performance cooperative group (top three to four students in a classroom) and differentiates the learning task and expectations for this group in specific academic subject area.
• Cross-graded classes	Students are "sent" to the appropriate grade level for specific subject instruction according to their current performance level (e.g., fourth-grade student goes to sixth-grade classroom for math).

Any way we look at it, there is a menu of grouping options that provide substantial positive outcomes for learners with gifts and talents, and we haven't even touched on *what* will be offered in the grouped setting or *how* instruction will be delivered. Perhaps James Kulik said it best all those years ago as he summarized his own meta-analyses on grouping (1992):

> The questions that people ask about grouping are not easy to answer. Do children benefit from it? Who benefits most? Does grouping harm anyone? How? Why? The answers depend on the type of grouping program. Results differ in programs that (a) group students by aptitude but prescribe a common curriculum for all groups; (b) group students by aptitude and

prescribe different curricula for the groups; and (c) place highly talented students into special enriched and accelerated classes that differ from other classes in both curricula and other resources. Benefits from the first type of program are positive but very small. Benefits from the second type are positive and larger. Benefits from the third type of program are positive, large, and important. (pp. xv–xvi)

Karen B. Rogers, Ph.D.
Professor of Gifted Studies
University of St. Thomas, College of Applied Professional Studies

Conclusion

Teachers must want to differentiate or they won't do it, at least not often. Teachers most likely will be motivated by knowing it is best for their students—that differentiating is the only way to engage all students in learning and to ensure that each student makes continuous progress.

No strategy is implemented as easily the first time as it is after repeated use. Keep up the good work of differentiating and bring more and more strategies into your repertoire, strategies that allow you to differentiate. It will be worth the effort and get easier each time you use the strategies in your toolbox. More students will be engaged in learning, so students win and so do you.

Survival Tips

- Parents must be provided with information on differentiation so they will understand that all students will not be completing identical assignments. They can begin to "get it" when you explain that all children in your class don't wear the same size of shoe, and their experiences, interests, and levels of readiness vary as well. The one-size-fits-all curriculum is a misfit just as one size of shoe would be.

- Differentiate from the beginning of the year so students in your class won't expect everyone to be on the same page or doing the same learning experiences. After all, doing the same thing will result in some students finding school too easy and some too hard. Each one needs the "just right" level of learning to make continuous progress.

Survival Toolkit

- *Differentiating Instruction: Meeting Students Where They Are* (http://www.glencoe.com/sec/teachingtoday/subject/di_meeting.phtml): This website provides an overview of differentiation and several examples of what teachers should and should not do to differentiate effectively.

- *Differentiated Instruction for Young Gifted Children: How Parents Can Help* (http://www.nagc.org/uploadedFiles/PHP/PHP_Article_Archive/2004/Sept/Differentiated%20for%20Young-Parents%20Can%20Help-Smutny-9_04PHP.pdf): This article, while directed toward parents, provides several examples of how differentiation is used with young gifted children.

- *What Every Parent Should Know About Differentiated Instruction* (http://www.dukegiftedletter.com/articles/vol9no1_connex.html): This column is a good resource to provide to parents who have questions about differentiation in the classroom.

- Carr, M. A. (2009). *Differentiation made simple: Timesaving tools for teachers.* Waco, TX: Prufrock Press.

- Karnes, F. A, & Stephens, K. R. (2010). *The ultimate guide for student product development and evaluation* (2nd ed.). Waco, TX: Prufrock Press.

- Tomlinson, C. A. (1999). *The differentiated classroom: Responding to the needs of all learners.* Upper Saddle River, NJ: Prentice Hall.

- Tomlinson, C. A. (2004). *How to differentiate instruction in mixed-ability classrooms* (2nd ed.). Alexandria, VA: Association for Supervision and Curriculum Development.

- Westphal, L. (2007). *Differentiating instruction with menus: Language arts.* Waco, TX: Prufrock Press.

- Westphal, L. (2007). *Differentiating instruction with menus: Math.* Waco, TX: Prufrock Press.

- Westphal, L. (2007). *Differentiating instruction with menus: Science.* Waco, TX: Prufrock Press.

- Westphal, L. (2007). *Differentiating instruction with menus: Social studies.* Waco, TX: Prufrock Press.

14 Excellence: An Important But Elusive Goal in Schools

This report is intended to provide some preliminary excellence gap data and kick start the national discussion on the importance of excellence in our national and state K–12 education systems.—Plucker, Burroughs, and Song (2010, p. 1)

Key Question

- What does excellence look like for elementary, middle, and high school students in this age of proficiency?

Excellence seems to be much like motherhood and apple pie. How could anyone oppose such a concept? Yet excellence is often supported selectively in our schools, communities, and nation. Frequently, people cheer for excellence in sports. People are likely to support excellence in the arts. Yet it is very important, actually essential, for excellence to be the goal set for children at all grade levels, by all educators. Excellence must be the goal of education for all children—including those who are gifted and talented.

Excellence in U.S. Schools

The report *National Excellence: A Case for Developing America's Talent* (U.S. Department of Education, 1993), the second national report on gifted education, stated:

> In a broad range of intellectual and artistic endeavors, America's most talented students often fail to reach their full potential . . . They are often tenacious in pursuits that interest them. The way in which they learn sets them apart from most other children and challenges educators and parents. (p. 5)

This report described "a silent crisis in educating talented students" in the United States, silent in that the effects of not developing the potential of advanced learners will not be felt for another generation (p. 5). In this silent crisis, "the talents of disadvantaged and minority children have been especially neglected" (p. 5).

Excellence has taken a backseat to proficiency with the No Child Left Behind (2001) legislation. Loveless, Farkas, and Duffett (2008) reported that "teachers are much more likely to indicate that struggling students, not advanced students, are their top priority" (p. 4). With the emphasis on bringing all children to proficiency, Loveless and colleagues found that "while the nation's lowest-achieving youngsters made rapid gains from 2000 to 2007, the performance of top students was languid" (p. 2). *Languid* is a word that you would hardly want to be the descriptor of achievement for high-ability children, nor is it a word that you would choose to describe your hoped-for future.

Mind the (Other) Gap is a report on the excellence gap that was released in February of 2010. In this report, Plucker, Burroughs, and Song delivered the strong message that there is an excellence gap in the United States, one that is infrequently mentioned. One suggestion in the report is that two questions should be asked when decisions are made for the classroom, school, or district:

1. How will this [decision] affect our brightest students?
2. How will this [decision] help other students begin to achieve at high levels? (p. 30)

These questions would raise the level of awareness of the impact of classroom and school decisions on removing the learning ceiling. Excellence is out of reach for children when the learning ceiling is low, and certainly when the ceiling is placed at grade level, which is the bar for proficiency. As John M. Bridgeland, coauthor of *Achievementrap: How America Is Failing Millions of High-Achieving Students From Lower-Income Families* (Wyner, Bridgeland, & DiIulio, 2007), stated in 2007, "These extraordinary students are found in every corner of America and represent the American dream. They defy the stereotype that poverty precludes high achievement. Notwithstanding their talent, our schools are failing them every step of the way" (para. 9).

The first recommendation by the National Science Board (2010) is to "provide opportunities for excellence":

> We cannot assume that our Nation's most talented students will succeed on their own. Instead, we must offer coordinated, proactive, sustained formal and informal interventions to develop their abilities. Students should learn at a pace, depth, and breadth commensurate with their talents and interests and in a fashion that elicits engagement, intellectual curiosity, and creative problem solving—essential skills for future innovation. (p. 2)

Students from low-income families consistently underachieve in schools, regardless of the grade level. One solution offered in *Achievementrap* was that "Educators must raise their expectations for lower income students and implement effective strategies for maintaining and increasing advanced learning within this population" (Wyner et al., 2007, p. 7). Teachers must have high expectations for all of their students regardless of their background.

How important is excellence in your school? Isn't excellence the goal for the basketball and soccer teams in your school? Hopefully, academics also have excellence as the desired goal throughout your school. What does excellence look like in science, social studies, language arts, and mathematics, as well as in the visual and performing arts?

Thomas Friedman (2010) implored all of society to get involved in a push for excellence in a *New York Times* article:

> Finally, just when globalization and technology were making the value of higher education greater than ever, and the price for lacking it more punishing than ever, America started slipping behind its peers in high school graduation rates, college graduation, and global test scores in math and critical thinking.
>
> Beyond the recession, this triple whammy is one of the main reasons that middle-class wages have been stagnating. To overcome that, we need to enlist both the U.S.G. [U.S. government] and the P.T.A. We need teachers and principals who are paid better for better performance, but also valued for their long hours and dedication to students and learning. We need better parents ready to hold their kids to higher standards of academic achievement. We need better students who come to school ready to learn, not to text. And to support all of this, we need an all-society effort—from the White House to the classroom to the living room—to nurture a culture of achievement and excellence. (para. 6 & 8)

Figure 15. There's no heavier burden than a great potential. Reprinted with permission. Peanuts: 2010 Peanuts Worldwide LLC., dist by UFS, Inc.

Conclusion

The Peanuts cartoon in Figure 15 raises the idea that there is no heavier burden than having a great potential. Think about the last frame in this cartoon. What a powerful message it includes. It is a message that needs to be kept in mind as you work with children who are gifted and talented. Remember that much of the public and many educators believe firmly that gifted children will make it on their own, so you don't need to worry about them. Of course, giving gifted children opportunities to fulfill their great potentials is the overarching goal of this book. It is a survival guide for teachers so that they will have the information and strategies to help children who are gifted and talented thrive—thereby developing their full potentials. The goal is to lighten the burden that having such potential has for some young people. They need to aim for excellence and to have learning opportunities to reach that high goal.

Survival Tips

- You must not lose sight of excellence in this age of proficiency.

- Parents need to know that proficiency is grade-level learning and that their children need to have excellence as their goal. They need to advocate for excellence, knowing that a school can bring children to proficiency who are not there yet and also teach children who have already gone beyond proficiency to levels of excellence.

Survival Toolkit

- Davidson, J., Davidson, B., & Vanderkam, L. (2005). *Genius denied: How to stop wasting our brightest young minds.* New York, NY: Simon & Schuster.

- Wyner, J. W., Bridgeland, J. M., & DiIulio, J. J. (2007). *Achievementrap: How America is failing millions of high-achieving students from lower-income families.* Landsdowne, VA: Jack Kent Cooke Foundation.

15 A Tough Choice for Some: An "A" Today or Preparation to Be Successful Tomorrow

All students need to break an academic sweat on a regular basis. No athlete who only breaks an athletic sweat occasionally will become a champion.—Julia L. Roberts and Julia Roberts Boggess

Key Question

- What is your personal definition of academic success?

Remember Friedman's (2010) call for "an all-society effort to nurture a culture of achievement and excellence" (para. 8)? Such a national effort requires teachers, parents, and students to answer the question: Which is more important—all A's today or being successful in postsecondary opportunities and careers tomorrow?

To a parent or teacher who knows the dangers that come from students earning easy A's, it is probably no decision at all. After all, a child's future is more important than any grade; however, many parents sabotage their child's academic future by complaining to the teacher that "You gave my child her first B" or "My child does not have any time for homework, as he is practicing soccer and involved with other afterschool activities every afternoon." Parents need to consider the child's future academic success as they examine what they

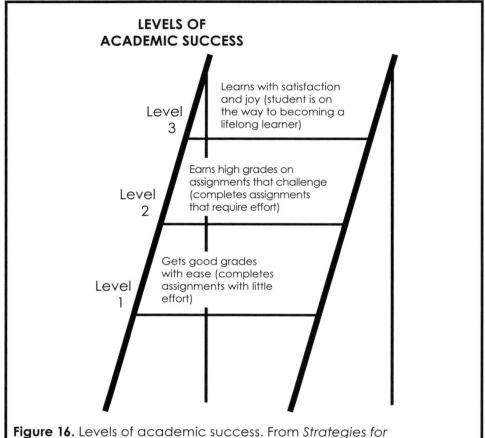

LEVELS OF ACADEMIC SUCCESS

Level 3 — Learns with satisfaction and joy (student is on the way to becoming a lifelong learner)

Level 2 — Earns high grades on assignments that challenge (completes assignments that require effort)

Level 1 — Gets good grades with ease (completes assignments with little effort)

Figure 16. Levels of academic success. From *Strategies for Differentiating Instruction: Best Practices for the Classroom* (2nd ed.), by J. L. Roberts and T. F. Inman, 2009, p. 14, Waco, TX: Prufrock Press. Copyright 2009 Prufrock Press. Reprinted with permission.

emphasize for their children today. Messages that are both spoken and implied will have a huge impact on academic preparation for being successful as learning experiences become more challenging.

What Is Academic Success?

One of the biggest problems for children who are gifted and talented is that educators and parents often equate excellence with straight A's or scores of 100. Unless a child works hard to earn the A or 100 (or close to that number), there is no move toward excellence, but rather she gets a reward for little or no effort. Learning needs to be the goal of school, with the ultimate goal of producing a lifelong learner. Figure 16 displays the levels of learning. The bottom rung is a risky place for a child to be, at least for very long, because he will get accustomed to "easy" work that often is done quickly. Before long, easy work is expected, and when assignments take time and thought, many gifted students doubt whether they are capable or not. That is when underachievement sets in, and underachievement is difficult to reverse. Excellence cannot be equated to A's unless the young person is challenged to earn the A.

What is your personal definition of academic success? Your answer to this question will determine your approach to teaching in general and to differentiation specifically.

A big question: Can you have both equity and excellence? If you think of equity not as everyone doing the same thing, but rather as each student making continuous progress, then excellence is a target that can be reached.

Children develop expectations that school may be equated with "easy" if they are not required to engage in challenging learning every day at school. Parents who rebuff a teacher for preparing challenging learning experiences, indicating a preference for all A's rather than important learning, often get what they ask for—easier work for their children. Teachers may decide that it is not worth the effort to buck parents' objections to the challenging work that they plan. Who loses when that happens? The child for sure—and, Friedman argued, the nation as well.

Academic Challenge as the Key for Future Success

What should you know in order to understand why challenging academic work is the foundation of success in postsecondary education?

1. Schools should provide ongoing opportunities for each child to make continuous progress, which translates to learning on an ongoing basis. A child who is reading at a level above his grade should be reading at another year or higher level by the end of the school year. A child should be learning more advanced math each year, no matter what the curriculum is for her grade level. Imposing ceilings on what a child who is advanced can learn in school stifles her academic progress and paves the way for underachievement.

2. Recent ACT reports (Gewertz, 2010) revealed that only 23% of the graduating seniors taking the ACT last year had scores that indicated that they were "college ready" in all four content areas that the ACT assesses—math, English, reading, and science. Arriving at college without adequate preparation places a young person in a hazardous position.

3. Children who find A's easy to gain often get into a pattern of underachievement that is hard to reverse. Underachievement is a pervasive problem. (See Chapter 21.)

Do you know anyone who excels as an adult who does not have a strong work ethic in his area of expertise? A work ethic usually develops during a child's early years. It is very difficult, if not impossible, to work hard at something you already have mastered at the level that instruction is being delivered. Easy schoolwork deprives a child of the opportunity to work hard to accomplish learning goals that are challenging. The child does not learn to be resilient or to set challenging goals. How much better would it be for the student to arrive at college with a strong preparatory background as he embarks upon what a parent hopes will be a college career that culminates in graduation?

Barriers to Academic Success

What actions create barriers that prevent children from being prepared for success in postsecondary education?
1. Parents rescue the student when the class seems difficult for fear the child will not have straight A's.
2. Schools are not offering challenging learning experiences in all classes at all levels—kindergarten through the senior year.
3. Students are not choosing the rigorous classes that are available.
4. Students are not developing a work ethic related to academics. Either classes lack the rigor to require hard work or the student has not devoted both time and energy necessary to develop a strong work ethic.

The country needs to embark on a major public relations campaign that encourages parents and educators to support children in working hard to meet challenging academic goals and to develop talent. A catchy slogan would help carry the message. School newsletters should carry information to help parents understand the great need to support their children as they work hard to reach important goals in their schoolwork. Nothing short of that will turn around the focus on grade-level curriculum as the standard fare for all children in a certain age range. Instead, we need to focus on nurturing lifelong learners who are ready to problem solve and make ethical decisions. All A's on grade-level assignments won't keep our country in a competitive status.

A Very Important Question

A great question to ask in order to get educators and parents thinking about why academic challenge is critical for developing lifelong learners follows:

If during the first 5 or 6 years of school, a child earns good grades and high praise without having to make much effort, what are all of the things he doesn't learn that most children learn by third grade?

Take a few minutes to answer that question. Even better, gather together others on your faculty to generate responses to this question. For many educators and parents, this question brings the first realization that children who are advanced are actually hindered in their academic and social development when they don't have academic challenges as a regular part of their learning. Some of the important learning that doesn't happen when school is easy and praise is frequent includes resilience, persistence, problem-solving skills, ability to deal with disappointment (maybe even creating a sense of failure in the student when he receives a B instead of an A), and study skills. To top that list off, the children haven't developed a work ethic either. It isn't possible to build a work ethic without learning opportunities that involve challenge. Then, ask your colleagues to make generalizations based on this discussion. For many educators, the opportunity to discuss what students have not learned will be their first time to consider how bright students are harmed when they are not challenged. What an important realization that is! It is a motivator for teachers to differentiate from the day that children start school. After you have engaged in discussing this very important question, pass out the article by Tracy Inman in the Survival Toolkit for this chapter on what students don't learn.

Effort and Motivation Matter!

Reis and Renzulli (2009) highlighted the importance of effort and motivation, adding an exclamation point to their summarization of these two concepts.

> *Effort and motivation matter!* No single non-cognitive trait is more influential on higher levels of performance than effort or motivation, and in addition to factors mentioned above, young people and adults with high potential are most hampered by underchallenging learning or work experiences. High-aptitude students often "coast" through school without having to expend effort, and when they finally *do* encounter a challenge, some experience a loss of confidence in their abilities resulting in diminished achievement levels (Reis & McCoach, 2000). (p. 234)

Carol Dweck (2006) described mindsets in two categories—those that are fixed and those that have a growth mindset. Students with a fixed mindset believe that being smart means they just need to show or demonstrate their abilities. In contrast, those students with a growth mindset know they need to work hard to get the best results. If they aren't successful at something (for example, they don't do well on a test), they figure out what they need to do in order to not have that occur the next time. Successful people have a growth mindset. On the other hand, a student with a fixed mindset who does poorly on a test will see herself as being not as smart as she thought she was. Providing feedback on effort the student made or didn't make reinforces for the young person that she is in charge of her future. The effort she puts into a project makes a huge difference in the assessment of the project. Mindsets are formed early in life, but they can be changed with concentrated effort.

Conclusion

A very important question for parents to answer is "What do I consider to be academic success for my children?" Educators need to educate parents concerning the critical need for young people to acquire the motivation and skills to be lifelong learners. Educators also need to challenge all children, including those who are gifted and talented, so that they know how to break an academic sweat. Being successful in postsecondary opportunities and later in careers depends on a strong work ethic, perseverance, and lifelong learning skills. Real academic success depends upon having a learning opportunity that the young person isn't quite sure he can accomplish, with the end result of reaching that goal by working hard.

Survival Tips

- Parents and educators need to understand what their children will face when they are not prepared to meet academic challenge. Eventually that challenge will come and a great grade point average won't help them.

- This message may be the most important one of all for parents: They must understand that making top grades without academic challenge results in young people who are unprepared for success in postsecondary opportunities.

Survival Toolkit

- *Best Motivation Video Ever* (http://www.youtube.com/watch?v=Rm Txr7OsPj0&feature=related): This Youtube video tells of several well-known people who suffered huge disappointments and overcame them. It is a great discussion starter with young people.

- *What a Child Doesn't Learn* (http://www.wku.edu/Dept/ Support/AcadAffairs/Gifted/giftedsite/wordpress/wp-content/ uploads/2010/07/Challenge181.pdf): This article by Tracy Inman, in *The Challenge*, the magazine of The Center for Gifted Studies at Western Kentucky University, discusses the things children who expect to get easy A's don't learn in school, like work ethic, time management, goal setting, and study skills.

16 Encourage Creativity: The Edge for the Future

Creativity is far more than just the generation of new ideas or the production of artistic works. It is a way of thinking *and* a comprehensive ongoing process *that involves multiple types of thinking, working, revising, producing, and evaluating.* —Tamara Fisher, a K–12 gifted education specialist for a school district in northwest Montana and President of the Montana Association of Gifted and Talented Education

Key Question

- What ongoing opportunities for creative thinking do children and young people have in your classroom and school, and how do you encourage creativity?

Creativity is a very important topic today, one being discussed by leaders in business and industry. Creative breakthroughs often fuel the economy. Moving forward economically depends on innovation. As Thomas Friedman (2009) stated

> The country that uses this crisis to make its population smarter and more innovative—and endows its people with more tools and basic research to invent new goods and services—is the one that will not just survive but thrive down the road. (para. 3)

What does innovation have to do with gifted education? There are several connections. Individuals who are gifted and talented will not be the only innovators; however, they have exceptional potential to have great ideas that lead to innovations. On the other hand, the potential to innovate is often stifled when creativity is not modeled or encouraged.

Sometimes creativity has not just been ignored but actively discouraged in the race for proficiency testing. Yet the future depends upon creative individuals and their ideas. As they saying goes, "All music was once new." The same is true with all ideas. As a teacher, you foster creativity when you encourage, expect, and respect creative responses.

Creativity—What Is It?

One of the challenges with creativity is knowing what it is—what does creativity look like when you see it? Treffinger (2009) asked what creativity means to educators: "Does it refer to artistic ability, to a set of cognitive skills, or to inventiveness or imagination?" (p. 245). Of course, creativity can be evidenced in all of those dimensions. A teacher who places a premium on creativity will be looking for creative responses in answers, questions, and a variety of products.

Myths about creativity abound. Many people misunderstand what creativity looks like and think that creativity is mainly found among artists. Of course, artists are creative, but creativity also describes thinking that can be done in science, language arts, history, and mathematics. Many educators think they are encouraging creativity if the student writes a poem, paints a picture, or performs a skit. Those products can be creative, but they are not necessarily so. Creativity is evidenced in ideas as well as in products. Young people must be encouraged to think about ideas in fresh ways and to process their thinking from a new perspective or vantage point.

Strategies to Foster Creativity

Remain Neutral in Responses

When leading a discussion in which you want creative responses, you need to remain fairly neutral. If you were to respond, "That is a great idea," others may be cautious about entering the conversation. Likewise, they may be reluctant to risk offering a creative idea if someone else's idea had been greeted with an unfavorable response. Keep the discussion going with comments such as "That's one response" or "What is another way that the same thing could be accomplished?"

Include Creativity in the Rubric

Be sure to include creativity in the rubric for a product. The DAP Tool (Roberts & Inman, 2009a) uses creativity as one of four components to guide students in completing products and you, the teacher, in assessing the products (see Figure 17). The other four components of the DAP Tool are content, presentation, and reflection. Teamed with creativity, those four components are the same, with only the presentation component changing as the product changes. Consequently, the DAP Tool is a protocol to guide students as they develop products and teachers as they assess them. Too often, student products will be more similar than different unless creativity is one expectation that you specify for the students to address. Students will know you expect them to be creative about their work if you include it as a component in the rubric.

Teach Creativity Thinking Skills

Ensure that the children know creative thinking skills (i.e., fluency, flexibility, originality, and elaboration) and can apply them. They need to know what each creative thinking skill is and how to incorporate these skills as they write, think about content, and complete project-based learning.

Bring Individuals Who Value Creativity into the Classroom

Bring in individuals from business and industry, as well as the arts, to talk about creativity and how important it is in their lives—professional and otherwise. Make as many connections as you can for the students—connections between their interests and goals and creativity.

Provide Time to Nurture Creativity

Give students time to be creative. In a short time it is easy to answer who, what, when, and where questions, but it takes time to wonder and reflect in order to produce more creative ideas on a topic.

Reward Creativity

Reward creativity on an ongoing basis, and let students know that being creative is important. Too often creative ideas and questions are discouraged with comments such as "We don't have time for that question now" or "Ask questions that stick to the facts."

POSTER Tier 2—DAP TOOL

CONTENT	• Content is accurate.	0 1 2 3 4 5 6
	• Content has depth and complexity of thought.	0 1 2 3 4 5 6
	• Content is organized.	0 1 2 3 4 5 6
PRESENTATION		
TEXT	• Title enhances the poster's purpose and is well placed. Text highlights most important concepts in topic.	0 1 2 3 4 5 6
GRAPHICS	• Graphics (illustrations, photos) add information and are appropriate for the topic.	0 1 2 3 4 5 6
LAYOUT	• Layout design clearly emphasizes graphics in an organized and attractive manner. Text is placed to clearly describe/explain all graphic images. Spacing is carefully planned with consideration of space not used.	0 1 2 3 4 5 6
CREATIVITY	• Individual insight is expressed in relation to the content.	0 1 2 3 4 5 6
	• Individual spark is expressed in relation to the presentation.	0 1 2 3 4 5 6
REFLECTION	• Reflection on the learning of the content through product development is apparent.	0 1 2 3 4 5 6
	• Reflection on what the student learned about self as a learner is apparent.	0 1 2 3 4 5 6

Comments

_____

_____

Meaning of Performance Scale:
6—PROFESSIONAL LEVEL: level expected from a professional in the content area
5—ADVANCED LEVEL: level exceeds expectations of the standard
4—PROFICIENT LEVEL: level expected for meeting the standard
3—PROGRESSING LEVEL: level demonstrates movement toward the standard
2—NOVICE LEVEL: level demonstrates initial awareness and knowledge of standard
1—NONPERFORMING LEVEL: level indicates no effort made to meet standard
0—NONPARTICIPATING LEVEL: level indicates nothing turned in

Figure 17. Poster tier 2–DAP tool. From *Assessing Differentiated Student Products: A Protocol for Development and Evaluation,* by J. L. Roberts and T. F. Inman, 2009, p. 142, Waco, TX: Prufrock Press. Copyright 2009 Prufrock Press. Reprinted with permission.

Be Open to Surprises

Be open to surprise findings. The 2010 Nobel Prize in physics was awarded to Andre Geim and Konstantin Novoselov for discovering graphene, the thinnest and strongest substance yet known. The discovery of graphene was the result of an unexpected discovery (see http://nobelprize.org/nobel_prizes/physics/laureates/2010 for the story). Examples like this one can help students value creative thinking skills like brainstorming and trial and error.

Let Students Learn About Creative Thinkers

Expose your students to creative thinkers through biographies, films, and stories about discovery. Guest speakers can also help in this aspect. Remember that professionals from many different fields, including business and industry, employ creative thinking to solve everyday problems.

Expect Creativity in All Disciplines

Remember that creativity is not limited to the visual and performing arts. Creative ideas are to be encouraged and expected in all content areas.

Watch for Signs of Creativity

Not only is it important for you to encourage creative thinking, you also must be watching for signs of creativity. One early sign of creative thinking is using something in a way other than its intended use. As one example, the child finds a LEGO piece to substitute for a person as he tells a story with prompts. Or another student may choose to substitute a new material to improve a product.

Synectics

Another way to encourage creative thinking is to use synectics. William Gordon (1961) defined synectics as "the joining together of different and apparently irrelevant elements" (p. 1). He wrote that "synectics theory applies to the integration of diverse individuals into a problem-stating problem-solving group" (p. 1), and it includes combining ideas in a variety of ways. Gordon put together people from various disciplines in order to solve problems.

Synectics is based on metaphorical thinking. How is something like something else? Asking metaphorical questions stimulates young people to think at high levels. You might ask, "Your birthday is like what kind of flower and why?" Or you may ask, "What kind of weather is like exploration?" Of course, you always ask "why" to see what connection the student is making between the two items. These questions would not have a content base, but they would limber up the students' thinking abilities before using metaphorical thinking in a discussion. Wouldn't you stretch before doing physical exercise? The same is true for mental exercise.

One step in synectics is to look at compressed conflicts, which requires your students to look at words that don't seem to go together and to think of what they know that fits both descriptors. For example, "What do you know that is both delicate and strong or loved and dreaded?" A spider web, a parent's love, or an egg might be responses to the query of what is both delicate and strong, but they provide only the starting point of possibilities. Such questions provoke many responses that come from one's own experiences. Until you ask such questions, students may never stretch to think of something from two different perspectives.

The Creative Thinking Jot Down

Behaviors typical of creative thinkers are shown in the Creative Thinking Jot Down in Figure 18. You also can go back to Chapter 5 to see Table 1, which compares behaviors of high achievers, gifted learners, and creative thinkers.

Classroom teachers sometimes don't appreciate creative thinkers. Young students often ask a lot of questions that may not have ready answers. But stop and think for a minute. Good questions are really more important than right answers. Questions move thinking forward, whereas a right answer is simply a right answer. Good minds will move our society forward with new approaches and innovations. One of the best ways to encourage creative thinking is to show that you value good questions. In fact, you may encourage parents to ask their children at the end of a school day if they asked any good questions today. That type of thinking is very important.

The Innovation Wheel

In a magnet program that is part of Project Gifted Education in Mathematics and Science (GEMS), a partnership between The Center for Gifted Studies at Western Kentucky University and the Warren County Schools, innovation is the universal theme that guides the curriculum. Of course, innovation is a theme that could be applied across the curriculum. The heuristic in Figure 19 includes both critical and creative skills. Words were carefully chosen to encourage students to wonder, imagine, anticipate, revise, produce, and conceptualize. The figure illustrates various ways one thinks that lead to innovation; the beginning point is wondering.

The Innovation Wheel has been conceptualized to guide the questions of the teacher and the thinking of the students in ways that lead to creative approaches to content as well as to issues and problems related to the content. Each of the verbs requires thinking—inquire, create, analyze, enhance, communicate, and

Creative Thinking Jot Down

Brief description of
observed activity _____

Date ____ / ____ / ____
                  Mo.   Day   Yr.

Teacher _____
Grade _____ School _____

1. As students show evidence of the following creative thinking characteristics in comparison with age peers, jot their names down in the appropriate box/es.
2. When recommending students for gifted services, use this identification jot down as a reminder of student performances as creative thinkers.

Offers many ideas (fluency).	Displays ability to switch categories or change ideas (flexibility).	Develops ideas with details (elaboration).	Offers ideas no one else may have thought of (originality).
Asks questions about everything and anything (alert and curious).	Appears bored with routine tasks and may refuse to complete them.	Uses imaginative and a strong sense of fantasy.	Appears to be daydreaming at times.

Figure 18. Creative thinking jot down. From *Jot Downs* by M. A. Evans & L. Whaley (n.d.), unpublished manuscript, The Center for Gifted Studies, Western Kentucky University, Bowling Green, KY. Reprinted with permission of the authors.

Figure 18, continued

May be uninhibited with ideas or opinions; is sometimes radical or tenacious in expressing ideas.	Is a high risk taker with an adventurous and speculative spirit.	Has high energy level that may cause the student to get in trouble.	Sees humor in situations others do not see (keen sense of humor).
Offers ideas others may view as wild and crazy.	May not read rules or may question the rules.	Enjoys spontaneous activities; sometimes without considering the consequences.	Appears reflective or idealistic.

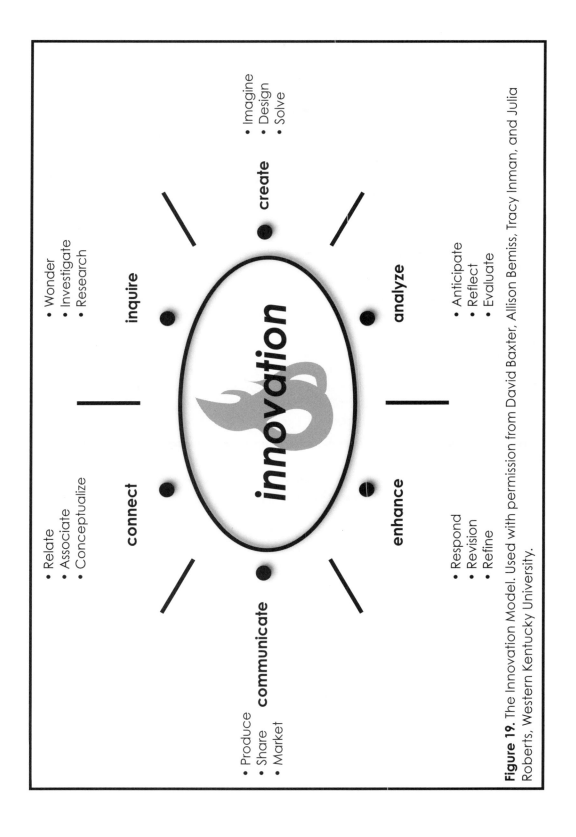

Figure 19. The Innovation Model. Used with permission from David Baxter, Allison Bemiss, Tracy Inman, and Julia Roberts, Western Kentucky University.

connect. There is really no starting or stopping point on the wheel. It is intended that each step in the process will be repeated as the innovation process continues.

Conclusion

Creativity is vitally important for the future. Consequently, it is critical that creative thinking is not only encouraged but also expected in assignments of various products. Too often educators expect creativity to be the domain of the visual and performing arts. Instead, creativity should be noticed and rewarded in all content areas.

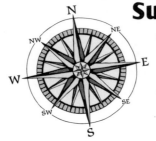

Survival Tips

- As you nurture and encourage creative thinking, you are preparing designers, inventors, and entrepreneurs of the future.

- Parents need to know that creativity is going to be a key factor in the future success of their child. In a world in which you can search Google for answers, it will be the creative problem solvers who will likely be most successful in their careers.

Survival Toolkit

- *Invention Convention* (http://library.thinkquest.org/J002783/InvCon. htm): This is a website by creative kids for other creative kids, offering various resources on creativity.

- *The Torrance Center* (http://www.coe.uga.edu/torrance): The Torrance Center at the University of Georgia is dedicated to creativity and carrying out the mission established by the work of E. Paul Torrance. The center offers professional development and special events dedicated to creativity.

- Cramond, B. (2005). *Fostering creativity in gifted students*. Waco, TX: Prufrock Press.

- Smutny, J. F., & van Fremd, S. E. (2009). *Igniting creativity in gifted learners, K–6*. Thousand Oaks, CA: Corwin Press.

17 Nurturing Leaders: A Necessity, Not an Option

The very essence of leadership is that you have to have vision. You can't blow an uncertain trumpet.—Theodore M. Hesburgh

Key Question

- What is the conceptualization of leadership that guides leadership training at your school?

Gifted children will not be the only leaders of the future, but they all will have opportunities to lead in their areas of expertise. The key is to provide experiences that will prepare them to be moral and effective leaders. They need to be resilient leaders, ones who can problem solve. Some will come with natural leadership ability, but all will need opportunities for leadership skills to be nurtured on an ongoing basis.

Leadership is optimally developed when there is an agreed-upon model of leadership that focuses on the skills of effective leaders. Without such a focus for leadership development in a classroom and school, providing experiences that could develop effective leaders is a hit-or-miss proposition. The uncertainty of reaching that destination is reminiscent of *Alice's Adventures in Wonderland* (Carroll, 1865/2000) when the Cheshire Cat tells Alice that if you don't know where you are going, any road will get you there. Having an agreed-upon destination enhances the possibility of getting there.

The Leadership to Make a Difference Model

The Leadership to Make a Difference Model, developed by Roberts (2010; see Figure 20), provides an array of skills that are important for effective leadership practice. There are numerous ways to teach and reinforce each of these skills in the classroom as well as in school and extracurricular activities. However, without a focus on specific skills, activities commonly done in the name of leadership development may miss the mark. Not only should the activities have a skill or skills as their goal, but discussion should both precede and follow any learning experiences with leadership skills embedded. Others may call the discussions debriefings. Questions can address how nonverbal communication was perceived, how planning could have been more effective, and so on. The purpose would be to develop leaders who will make a positive difference in their communities and beyond.

One expert, Mariam G. MacGregor, describes leadership development and suggests opportunities to ensure that young people learn about becoming effective leaders.

◇◇

SURVIVAL SECRETS FOR DEVELOPING STUDENTS' LEADERSHIP SKILLS

Mariam G. MacGregor

Educators have a responsibility to support leadership development in younger generations. Yet many schools and communities overlook practical ways to promote these lifelong skills. There are abundant opportunities to incorporate leadership development, ranging from leadership classes to mentoring and service-learning activities, integrating leadership across the curriculum, and engaging youth in decisions that positively affect school and community culture. Fortunately, these efforts can often be accomplished within the context of existing instructional minutes. And they can stretch from kindergarten to graduation!

Young people don't refer to textbook definitions or leadership theories to explain what it means to be a leader. Their

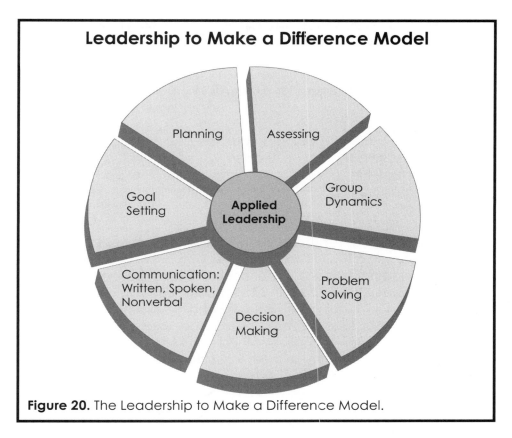

Figure 20. The Leadership to Make a Difference Model.

perspective (as with those of adults) can be captured by exploring this fundamental question:

> Would you be your own next-door neighbor? Would you give a house key to the "you" next door, trusting yourself to be responsible for your "neighbor's" house, children, pets, and monetary valuables?

Whether failing or making straight A's at school, troubled or not—young people's responses consistently demonstrate a profound understanding that it's not what people see on the outside that influences their actions, attitudes, and character, but it's who they are on the inside. Whether someone admits a willingness to live next door to herself or not, everyone benefits from having others who will intentionally tend to their leadership skills and attitudes so she is a "good neighbor."

Even in those perceived as being natural leaders, leadership skills left untended will not blossom. In fact, leadership talent applied without guidance or limits can produce lenient leaders, unconcerned with unethical, immoral, unwise, or arbitrary behaviors. However, leadership cultivated intentionally with deliberate training and support from a young age creates extraordinary individuals others want to follow.

Leadership is as much an attitude as it is a set of skills. By accepting this notion, leaders will be seen all around us—in fact, they *are* us—in everyday settings, not powerful positions, free of publicity and special attention, but no less important.

Good leaders can be easily overlooked because bad leaders call attention to themselves with brash errors and poor judgment. To find good leaders, we are reminded to look beyond the loudest and most boisterous people to find those quietly leading with integrity and humility. These are the everyday leaders, who possess clear expectations for their own behavior and how others should be treated, and who inspire those around them to set high standards as well.

Educators capable of nurturing *all* leadership abilities (latent and obvious) in their classrooms demonstrate good leadership. Educators willing to relinquish power so students take action, express their opinions, and influence sustainable change are good leaders. Educators capable of drawing out the shy, underestimated kids as equally as they do the extroverted ones are good leaders.

Exceptional leaders are the educators who model for *all* students what it means to lead and succeed at one's highest level; who challenge and prod students regardless of individual abilities, limitations, or self-doubt; and who expect students to become true leaders in return.

Mariam G. MacGregor
Founder and Director
Youthleadership.com
Denver, CO

Identifying Leadership Talent

How do you identify leadership talent? There are several possibilities, and they are most effective when used in combination. The Leadership Jot Down in Figure 21 focuses your attention on behaviors that are characteristic of leadership talent. Remember that no child shows evidence of all of the behaviors in a particular Jot Down, but rather the overall demonstration of behaviors typical of a child with leadership ability. Look for a pattern with a particular child's name being noted for demonstrating particular behaviors associated with leadership.

A leadership portfolio is a way to gather evidence of leadership potential and interest. The child, perhaps with the assistance of a teacher or counselor, puts together pieces that show his leadership interest and ability. These pieces could include reflections on leadership projects from school, youth organizations, or community activities. Letters from adults who have worked with the young person in activities outside the school would provide important information about a student's interest in leadership.

A sociogram (a graphic representation of a person's social links) can provide insight into whom the children in the class consider to be the leaders. A sociogram can be completed informally by asking students to anonymously answer questions like who they would they want to include in their group if they were completing a science project or designing a mural.

The *Everyday Leadership Skills and Attitudes Inventory* (MacGregor, 2010) is an assessment of one's leadership skills and attitudes. It provides the opportunity for self-assessment, as well as a means to measure growth in important leadership skills and change of attitudes.

Events to Showcase Learning About Leadership

Numerous experiences can be planned to showcase leadership learning, including the following suggestions.

- *An Evening of Notables.* Have a culminating activity in which students dress as a leader (current or historical) and carry on conversations in keeping with what they know about the individual historical figures.
- *Lunch With Leaders.* Invite community or school leaders in for lunch with your class. Have questions about leadership prepared beforehand to use in conversations with them. Students might enjoy having lunch with older student leaders (e.g., the student body president of your district's high school) and finding out how they developed their leadership skills.
- *Panel of Community Leaders.* Have leaders who represent various professions in the community serve on a panel. Ask them questions about

Leadership Jot Down

Date _____ / _____ / _____
Mo.   Day   Yr

Brief description of
observed activity _____

Teacher _____
Grade _____ School _____

1. As students show evidence of the following characteristics in comparison with age peers, jot their names down in the appropriate box/es.
2. When recommending students for gifted services, use this identification jot down as a reminder of student performances in leadership.

Is looked to by others when something must be decided.	Initiates activities that involve peers.	Figures out what is wrong with an activity and shows others how to make it better.
Judges abilities of others and finds a place for them.	May appear "bossy" at times.	Interacts easily with both children and adults.
Gets others to work toward desirable or undesirable goals.		
Transmits his or her enthusiasm for a task to others.		

Figure 21. Leadership jot down. From *Jot Downs* by M. A. Evans & L. Whaley (n.d.), unpublished manuscript, The Center for Gifted Studies, Western Kentucky University, Bowling Green, KY. Reprinted with permission of the authors.

| Is sought out by other students for play/activities. | Displays a sense of justice and fair play. | Organizes ideas and people to reach goal. | Displays self-confidence. |
| Is often the captain of teams or a leader in the classroom. | Displays charismatic qualities. | Communicates effectively to make things happen. | May be frustrated by lack of organization or progress toward goal. |

Figure 21, continued

leadership, including questions about their leadership roles when they were in elementary, middle, and high school.

Conclusion

The basic learning experiences that will develop leadership ability will have a focus on skills like communication and collaboration. Those experiences can be ongoing and occur in every classroom. The important thing to remember is to talk about how the various skills form the basis of what it means to be a leader.

Survival Tips

○ Leadership does not just develop, but rather it is nurtured. Educators can provide experiences that will help students learn to be outstanding leaders.

○ Young people need opportunities to hone their leadership skills as they set goals and work with others in order to reach their goals. Gifted children will grow up to be leaders in their professions, organizations, and communities. Make sure they are prepared to be effective leaders.

Survival Toolkit

○ Karnes, F. A., & Bean, S. M. (2010). *Leadership for students: A guide for young leaders* (2nd ed.). Waco, TX: Prufrock Press.

○ MacGregor, M. (2008). *Teambuilding with teens: Activities for leadership, decision making, & group success.* Minneapolis, MN: Free Spirit.

○ MacGregor, M. (2009). *Everyday leadership cards: Writing and discussion prompts.* Minneapolis, MN: Free Spirit.

18 Creating a Gold Standard School and District

Gold Standard Schools are places in which gifted children and young people thrive, but so do all other children.—Julia Roberts and Tracy Inman (2010, p. 21)

Key Question

- If you were to have the ideal situation, what services and opportunities would be in place in your classroom and school for students who are gifted and talented?

NAGC Pre-K–Grade 12 Gifted Programming Standards

As you work to improve services offered at your school, you need a target. The *NAGC Pre-K–Grade 12 Gifted Programming Standards: A Blueprint for Quality Gifted Education Programs* (NAGC, 2010a) will provide guidance for you and your colleagues to measure progress in terms of student outcomes. In fact, these standards can help you do the following:

- assess, evaluate, and improve local plans and programming;
- plan curriculum;
- provide professional development;

- advocate;
- develop, improve, and evaluate state standards; and
- approve gifted plans and programs and monitor for compliance with state regulations. (p. 4)

The six overarching standards included in the document include Learning and Development, Assessment, Curriculum Planning and Instruction, Learning Environments, Programming, and Professional Development. The standards document is available at http://www.nagc.org.

Checklist for the Gold Standard School

Another source to guide you is the checklist for a Gold Standard School (Roberts & Inman, 2010; see Figure 22). This checklist will assist you in planning for the learning needs of gifted students with fellow educators in your school and district.

You will be most effective in your role if you work well with others. Collaboration is key to improving student learning. Two experts discuss the topic of collaboration below: Mary Evans describes important considerations for working with your principal, and Virginia Burney highlights points to remember as you work with other teachers.

◇◇

SURVIVAL SECRETS FOR WORKING WITH YOUR PRINCIPAL

Mary Evans

The key to working with your principal effectively is communication. Set up a time to meet with your principal and ask what his or her vision is for gifted education at the school. Share your vision for what you want gifted education to look like in your school. What should the students, parents, classroom teachers, and administrators be doing in a school that meets the needs of gifted students? Volunteer to conduct a needs assessment to determine your school's level of implementation of best practices in gifted education.

Once the needs assessment has been conducted, discuss the results with the principal and ask to form a committee to review the data and set long- and short-term goals for the school. When principals understand their schools'

Gold Standard School Checklist

Characteristic 1: Focus on Continuous Progress

☐ 1.1 The school mission statement specifies that every child will realize his potential or each child will make continuous progress.

☐ 1.2 Preassessment is routine and establishes the interests, preferred ways of learning, and levels of readiness of all students.

☐ 1.3 Grouping for instructional purposes is a standard practice in order to facilitate all children (remember that includes gifted children) learning at appropriately challenging levels. Most groupings are flexible to allow students to be regrouped as the level of readiness changes with different content or topics as well as when interest shifts into high gear.

☐ 1.4 Assessment is ongoing to see that all children are learning. This type of assessment is called formative, and it is important because it monitors progress to make certain that a child is neither practicing skills incorrectly nor misunderstanding content.

☐ 1.5 Lessons are differentiated to match the level of challenge to the needs of individual students or clusters of students. Differentiated learning experiences are not "just different" nor are they simply more of the same.

Characteristic 2: Talent Development

☐ 2.1 Opportunities in a variety of content and talent areas are sought out, announced, and encouraged.

☐ 2.2 Achievements in a variety of content and talent areas are recognized and celebrated.

Characteristic 3: Policies That Remove the Learning Ceiling

☐ 3.1 A policy for acceleration is in place.

☐ 3.2 A policy for performance assessment is established.

☐ 3.3 A policy for educational enhancement is adopted.

☐ 3.4 Policies and practices do not inhibit continuous progress.

Characteristic 4: Ongoing Professional Development

☐ 4.1 Professional development about gifted education and talent development is embedded throughout a school year.

Figure 22. Gold standard school checklist. From "A Checklist to Guide Advocacy for a Gold Standard School," by J. L. Roberts and T. F. Inman, December 2010, p. 23, *Parenting for High Potential.* Copyright 2010 National Association for Gifted Children. Reprinted with permission.

needs, they will find ways to meet those needs, whether it is storage space, teaching space, help with scheduling, or additional resources. Professional development is frequently identified as a need. Talk to the principal about the ongoing professional development initiatives for the school and ways that gifted education can be integrated into those initiatives.

The gifted resource teacher is the only person in the building whose total focus is on gifted and talented education. Be positive, proactive, and always looking for ways to better serve gifted students. Volunteer to be on curriculum committees, nominate students and colleagues for awards, and offer to work a booth at the Fall Festival or open house events so that you are very visible in the building and seen as a dedicated member of the school team. Show your passion for meeting the needs of all students, including gifted students.

If you chair the building's gifted and talented committee, make sure the principal knows when the meetings are and receives an invitation to attend. Make sure he or she receives a copy of the agenda in advance of the meeting. Ask the principal to give a welcome speech when you hold parent meetings, brief the principal on parent concerns, and discuss solutions. Keep the principal well informed about the achievements of the gifted students, and ask the principal to help make students aware of opportunities that are available, such as Saturday enrichment classes, contests, programs at local museums, and so on. Offer to write a paragraph for the school newsletter about enrichment opportunities available in the community.

Collect quantitative and qualitative data to show the principal the value of gifted education for students. What percentage of identified students score at the highest level on the state assessment? Share what your students and parents are saying about the services provided. Take pictures and share them through a website. Include student quotes as captions to the pictures.

Communicate, communicate, communicate in every way you can so the principal has a full picture of the gifted students in the school. Find ways to show that raising the level of learning for gifted students raises the level of learning for all students.

Mary Evans, Ph.D.
Principal, Cumberland Trace Elementary School
Warren County Schools
Bowling Green, KY

◇◇

SURVIVAL SECRETS FOR GIFTED RESOURCE TEACHERS ON WORKING EFFECTIVELY WITH OTHER TEACHERS

Virginia Burney

The gifted resource teacher has the potential to transform education for gifted students and influence the faculty in terms of understanding the characteristics and needs of gifted students. You will share responsibility for the education of certain students, but you are also in a position to know what is going on in the classrooms of other teachers. The challenge is to establish positive relationships, trust, and clear expectations of the other faculty members. How can you do this?

Gain Clarity

Request a meeting with the district gifted coordinator and the principal to gain clarity on your role and its implementation. Before you meet, outline for yourself what you think that role is, your exact responsibilities, and how the logistics of sharing student instruction might be designed. This will help you clarify your own thinking and questions. During the meeting, the coordinator can clarify the district design for services, K–12, as well as offer suggestion for implementation. The principal will know the challenges and opportunities of the particular student population, faculty, and how the scheduling is to be organized. Together, develop written guidelines for what your role is so that other faculty can also have clarity. It will be time well spent and will establish the support of your principal and coordinator.

Offer to Assist and Establish Credibility

If you are already knowledgeable, offer to lead a book study or staff mini-lesson on some aspect of gifted education. Possible topics include the characteristics of gifted children, the social and emotional needs of this population, and differentiating to provide challenge. If you are not yet confident in your own knowledge, or if you want further development, ask the principal for support for your own professional development in gifted education. Ask to share in the schoolwide duties assigned to regular classroom teachers. Having bus duty, recess duty, cafeteria duty, and other responsibilities can demonstrate your competence in student management, makes you a member of the team, and provides you the opportunity to see the gifted students within the larger social milieu.

Establish Trust

Think of working with your colleagues in the same way we think of working with gifted children. Strive to understand both their cognitive and affective needs in order to be effective. Frame your work together as jointly influencing maximum growth in student achievement; this will establish common goals and benefits. Remember that it can be intimidating to other teachers for you to know so well what goes on in their classrooms. Be sensitive to that position, be positive about their strengths, share the joys and challenges of knowing the shared students, and be on the same team.

By establishing clear expectations for your role and the support of your administration, you should be in a position to establish your class or classroom support to maximum benefit. Seek to be a resource for the faculty as well as the students to gain team membership and leadership.

Virginia Burney, Ph.D.
Consultant, Indiana Department of Education; Instructor in Gifted Education,
Ball State University

Influencing Change

The *NAGC Pre-K–Grade 12 Gifted Programming Standards: A Blueprint for Quality Gifted Education Programs* (2010a) and the Gold Standard Schools checklist discussed earlier can give you some guidelines for what good gifted programs should encompass, but how do you go about making changes in your program or school? Expert Anita Davis provides guidance for upgrading your school district's services for gifted young people through her firsthand experiences in making changes to the gifted education policy in her district.

◇◇◇

SURVIVAL SECRETS FOR MAKING A DISTRICT OUTSTANDING IN GIFTED EDUCATION

Anita Davis

Our journey to change gifted education in our district started with the willingness to acknowledge the brutal facts presented by our parents, staff, and students. Dr. Phil's life law of "You can't change what you don't acknowledge" is so true, and until the leaders in our schools and district acknowledged that we were not providing the type of services our kids needed, no meaningful changes happened. Someone has to be willing to shine a light on what's happening and ask some hard questions. We were very fortunate to have a superintendent who did this in our district. If those at the top don't own the problem and make it a priority, it is nearly impossible to affect radical and evolutionary change (which is so desperately needed in many areas of K–12 education, especially gifted education).

But acknowledging the problem isn't enough—change comes only when folks roll up their sleeves and do something! We brought a task force together to analyze our current reality, study the research and best practices, and make recommendations about what needed to be done differently in our classrooms, schools, and district. The task force was comprised of representatives from our various stakeholders so that all had a voice in the process. The task force's first task was to articulate a vision statement, goals, and parameters for gifted education in our district. The committee then divided its findings and recommendations into five key areas: organization, identification, services, communication, and professional development. This report was shared with the board of education, which adopted the report as a multiyear action plan for immediate implementation. We now had the blueprint needed to build the type of gifted education services we envisioned.

At the same time the task force was working, administrative staff meetings were used to build shared knowledge about gifted education. All administrators were asked to do three things in relation to our study about gifted education: (1) be willing to be disturbed, (2) be willing to confront their biases, and (3) have a sense of urgency. We read numerous articles, examined the myths and truths about gifted students, looked at school through the eyes of our most capable students, and confronted some difficult realities about our practices and beliefs. Taking time to develop this type of understanding with our building and district leaders was pivotal and foundational to the change that ensued. They understood the vision and blueprint once it was presented to them by the task force and were better able to implement the recommendations in their respective buildings.

Throughout the process, the most critical factor that created understanding and ownership was our focus on always looking at things through the eyes of the gifted child. Putting folks in scenarios and making them see what the child experiences in the classroom and in life was extremely powerful. We knew that research and best practice appeal to the head, the rational, logical part of us all; we were committed to making sure we appealed to the heart as well, that part of us that drove us to be teachers.

Anita Davis
Assistant Superintendent, Curriculum and Instruction
Oldham County Schools
Buckner, KY

◇◇

Conclusion

Moving toward implementing programming standards characterized by best practices for all children, including those who are gifted and talented, will be easier when you have a clear target in mind and you have key educators and parents on board. Use the information in this chapter as your blueprint for what you want to put in place and how you should work to accomplish your goals.

Survival Tips

- Become very familiar with the *NAGC Pre-K–Grade 12 Gifted Programming Standards* and the components of a Gold Standard School to help determine changes that need to be made to your gifted program.

- Parents need to know what policies and practices could be in place in a school that would allow all students to thrive, including those who are gifted and talented. Such knowledge improves advocacy efforts by parents.

Survival Toolkit

- *NAGC PreK–Grade 12 Gifted Programming Standards* (http://www.nagc.org/index.aspx?id=546): This page includes a link to the downloadable booklet that outlines the latest standards created by the National Association for Gifted Children and The Association for the Gifted.

- Roberts, J. L., & Inman, T. F. (2010, December). A checklist to guide advocacy for a gold standard school. *Parenting for High Potential*, 21–23.

19 Making All Special Teachers the Gifted Child's Best Resources

Never apologize for talent! Talent is a gift! And that is my special talent, encouraging talent!—Madame Morrible in *Wicked: The Grimmerie: A Behind-the-Scenes Look at the Hit Broadway Musical*

Key Question

- In what ways can special teachers be talent developers for children and young people in your school?

Special teachers in your school will likely include the librarian, music teacher, art teacher, and physical education teacher. In middle school and high school you will also look to teachers of business, agriculture, and family and consumer sciences as resources, in addition to content teachers in core subjects. These teachers can be helpful resources to children who are gifted and talented, developing both interests and talents in their areas of expertise. Ongoing conversations between you and the special teachers can benefit the students who show special interests and talents in the teachers' areas of expertise. You and the special teachers can partner to see that talents blossom during each school year. They can give you suggestions and strategies for incorporating a talent area in your lesson plans for specific children with special interests or talents like art, music, dance, or the visual arts.

Working With the School Librarian

The school librarian usually has more resources at her disposal than any other person in the school. Becoming a lifelong learner requires accessing resources that allow a student to both answer and ask good questions. The librarian certainly will help students access resources for research, but she can facilitate learning in other ways as well.

For a librarian, working with gifted students can come in many different forms. Book studies with small groups provide an excellent opportunity for librarians to interact with gifted students. Often students are asked to focus on plot points or comprehension of reading materials in class. A book group will give the students a chance to focus on higher level thinking skills and delve into the complexities of a story or novel. Some great resources for finding appropriate reading material are:

- *Biographies for Talented Readers, A Bibliography* (http://www.ualr.edu/giftedctr/slufy/Biographies_for_Children.pdf): Ann Robinson at the University of Arkansas at Little Rock has put together this bibliography of biographies suitable for gifted children. The list includes the reading levels for each book.
- *Reading Lists* (http://www.hoagiesgifted.com/reading_lists.htm): The Hoagies' Gifted Education Page website provides several lists of recommended books for advanced readers on a variety of topics.
- Halsted, J. W. (2009). *Some of my best friends are books: Guiding gifted readers from preschool to high school* (3rd ed.). Scottsdale, AZ: Great Potential Press.
- Hauser, P., & Nelson, G. A. (1988). *Books for the gifted child* (Vol. 2). New York, NY: Bowker.

One challenge that many parents and teachers of gifted students face is finding material that is not only high-level reading, but high-interest and age-appropriate material. Librarians need to stay in tune with what students are interested in and update their collection with the needs and wishes of these children in mind. It is also important to mention that gifted students often prefer nonfiction books. Biographies are an excellent option to capture a gifted learner's interest.

Finding authors who write books that capture the interests of gifted students can be a challenge. Some authors we've found to be favorites of gifted kids include Lloyd Alexander, Jodi Lynn Anderson, Laurie Halse Anderson, Louise Arnold, E. D. Baker, Blue Balliett, Dave Barry, Ted Bell, Jeanne Birdsall, Pseudonymous Bosch, Berkeley Breathed, Georgia Byng, Beverly Cleary, Andrew Clements, Susan Cooper, Roald Dahl, Kate DiCamillo, Marguerite Henry, Anthony Horowitz, Polly Horvath, Erin Hunter, Brian Jacques, Robin Jarvis, Philip Kerr, E. L. Konigsburg, Madeleine L'Engle, Lois Lowry, Robert McCloskey, Marissa Moss,

Christopher Paolini, Gary Paulsen, Katherine Paterson, Rodman Philbrick, Ellen Potter, Guillaume Prevost, Rick Riordan, J. K. Rowling, Jon Scieszka, Lemony Snicket, Trenton Lee Stewart, Vivian Vande Velde, E. B. White, and Jane Yolen.

Bibliotherapy is an important way to help gifted students understand a variety of different issues that they may encounter. There are so many wonderful picture books that can help explore the social-emotional issues that gifted students experience. Don't let the term *picture books* limit their use to elementary children. In fact, some of these books are useful for getting important points about gifted children's needs understood by educators and parents, as well as by middle and high school students. Some favorites include:

- *Archibald Frisby* by Michael Chesworth (1996): This is an excellent book about a little boy whose mother worries that he is missing out on the rest of the world because he is too focused on science and reading. She ships him off to camp, where Archibald helps everyone at camp discover that science can be fun. It is a wonderful illustration of how gifted kids don't have to change to be happy.
- *The Big Orange Splot* by Daniel Pinkwater (1993): All of the houses in the neighborhood look exactly the same until one day a bird drops a can of orange paint on Mr. Plumbean's house. The neighborhood panics that his house looks different. Mr. Plumbean embraces the difference and uses his artistic abilities to create a multicolored masterpiece. Eventually the rest of the neighborhood realizes that creativity is better than conformity.
- *Eggbert, the Slightly Cracked Egg* by Tom Ross (1997): Even though he is a talented artist, Eggbert is banished from his home in the refrigerator when the other eggs discover he has a slight crack. Eggbert initially tries to disguise the fact that he is different, but eventually he discovers that there are many things in this world that are wonderful because they are different.
- *Ish* by Peter H. Reynolds (2004): Ramon loves creating art until his older brother teases him about his artwork. Ramon loses his passion for drawing until his younger sister shows him that art doesn't have to be perfect. This book is helpful for students who worry about perfection.
- *The Little Cupcakes* by Anthony King (2005): Caitlin is so excited to take cupcakes to school to share with her classmates. Some of the cupcakes have vanilla frosting and some have chocolate frosting. When the box is opened, the teacher decides to cut off all of the tops so that they will all be the same. When Caitlin returns home, devastated, her father comforts her by explaining that it is wonderful and important to celebrate all of the differences in the world. This book is a tale about the importance of diversity and tolerance.

- *Michael* by Tony Bradman (1997): Although Michael enjoys math, reading, art, and science, he does not enjoy how his teachers are teaching those subjects. Michael is considered by his teachers to be the "worst boy in school," and they do nothing to get him interested in school. Michael doesn't mind being unique and busies himself in each subject with his own projects. In the end, all of Michael's projects combine to surprise everyone with his accomplishment.
- *Odd Velvet* by Mary Whitcomb (1998): Velvet is a unique little girl who brings a milkweed pod to show-and-tell while other girls are bringing their dolls. When the other students first meet her, they think she is odd, but Velvet has great confidence in herself. Her confidence and her unique talents eventually win over her classmates.
- *Something Else* by Kathryn Cave (1998): A little creature is told by the other animals in town that he is not like them and that he "doesn't belong." He tries to fit in but to no avail. When another unique creature shows up at the door, Something Else initially rejects it, saying that it doesn't belong there. In the end, they become fast friends. This is a wonderful story about accepting each other's differences and a subtle nod to the Golden Rule.
- *Stand Tall, Molly Lou Melon* by Patty Lovell (2001): Molly Lou is a tiny, buck-toothed, clumsy first grader. Her grandmother gives her wonderful advice about embracing each of her unique characteristics. When she moves to a new school, she encounters a bully but rises above each of his insults with panache.
- *Violet: The Pilot* by Steve Breen (2008): Violet is different from her classmates because she prefers her set of tools to tea sets. She lives with her parents next to the junkyard and is a mechanical genius. As she grows up, her inventions become much more complex and often are flying machines. Her constant companion and only friend is her dog, Orville. Violet ignores the taunts of her classmates and instead focuses on creating a flying machine for the upcoming Air Show. As she travels to the Air Show in her new machine, she has to stop and rescue a Scout Troop. In the end, the town celebrates Violet's heroism, and Violet makes it on the cover of her favorite scientific magazine. This is a beautifully illustrated tale of a girl who is seen as different because she is passionate about science and engineering.

Working With the Art Teacher

Classroom teachers also need to recognize artistic talent and provide opportunities to highlight skills and interests in art as young people learn in other subject areas. Experts Judy Myers Bellemere and Mary Judith Bellemere Stallard provide suggestions for art teachers and classroom teachers to use to develop students' talent in art.

◇◇◇

SURVIVAL SECRETS FOR DEVELOPING ARTISTIC TALENT IN THE GIFTED CHILD

Judy Myers Bellemere and Mary Judith Bellemere Stallard

You not only have a room full of gifted children, each with special interests to address, but you discover that several are multitalented, little Leonardo da Vinci characters who create breathtaking pieces of art. The easy part is identifying the art talent. The harder part is encouraging development of the gift and broadening the scope. What to do?

The child who is gifted in art will be drawing at every possible moment, usually volunteers for any extra work having to do with art, and consistently creates art that catches the eye of the observer. He or she is able to combine the elements of design through drawing, painting, and three-dimensional projects in a way that delights the audience.

Three words to keep in mind when developing a student's artistic talent are not unlike those we pursue in any of the disciplines: expose, involve, affirm. The suggestions below could be workable for any age student, with teacher and parent support and approval.

- *Keep a journal, handmade or purchased.* This could be art for art's sake, or in conjunction with written dialogue. This should be the student's "personal playground," full of thumbnail sketches and notations on a variety of subjects. Notes can be made beside the drawings as to coloration, locality, and so on. It is good for kids to have one place where they feel they don't have to do a specific assignment and can express themselves fully. A teacher could interject a directed project, such as "Give me four sketches of an imaginary bug, or create a full page about your grandfather without drawing a person." Collage can be a part of the journal expressions. Containing some of the sketches in a linear rectangle or square can help with composition. Students can also choose a favorite sketch and from it develop a large, finished piece. Teachers can look at early works of esteemed artists with the students, and note that they seemed to master realistic depictions in their sketches before they began to explore the more abstract styles.

- *If you have a school art teacher, use her.* Ask if she provides enrichment for any of the children in an after-school program or pushes the depth of class projects for children with special ability.
- *Use your librarian.* Pull art appreciation books and biographies of artists from the library. Keep them out and available for the young artists to peruse. Have a student look at the drawings of Leonardo da Vinci, then have her stretch her own imagination and invent something that she will depict with similar fine draftsmanship.
- *Be sure to designate a special area for each artist's collection.* Encourage the student whose work you display to change it at will. For added affirmation, let him help design cover images and illustrations for teacher bulletins, class booklets, and other documents.
- *Include technique.* Provide more technical lessons, such as in-depth study as it relates to design and various media.
- *Provide variety and exposure.* Provide as much enrichment in as many of the visual art areas as possible. Students should visit galleries and *look at art*, old and new. Students should also watch artists making art. You can arrange this by enlisting the help of parents to take advantage of classes, workshops, and demonstrations offered by area galleries and artists.
- *Give art a purpose.* Take the students to see how and where art fits into a profession: architecture, advertising agencies, photography, galleries that handle sales for artists, functional and creative ceramic studios, the city's sculptures (which could lead to a trip to an area sculptor's studio), jewelry, computer graphics, cartooning, and illustration. Have them find an illustrator they like and embellish one of their own stories in a similar style.
- *Provide various mediums.* Keep a folder of art paper and different media accessible to the student. This opportunity could be accompanied by a list of suggested projects so that learning can take place, and the child can get beyond rainbows. Some suggested projects include:
  - Do figure sketches or gesture drawings of students making a presentation.

- Draw classmates at play or studying.
- After looking at classic drawing styles of great artists such as da Vinci, Rembrandt, or Degas, provide students with Conté crayons in terra cotta, grays, and blacks, and have them try to replicate the techniques as they draw their figures. Use the same technique with paintings: Show them a Wyeth watercolor, for example, and let them try to reproduce the painting, or a part of it, with their watercolors. This technique is a wonderful way for students to learn the possibilities of a certain media and how to achieve the varying effects.
- Show fine examples of cartooning, even political cartoons. Encourage development of students' own cartoon characters, and find a theme for their cartoons to follow. Let students place a cartoon in the weekly school newspaper or teachers' bulletins.
- Let talented students sketch a plan for a mural to be painted somewhere in the school. The plan should include a color study and layout. If approved, they could work on the mural during allocated time. A field trip to see other murals will be helpful.
- Advanced and mature students should consider enrolling in figure sketching classes, with parent approval.

In closing, let us say that to keep the young artist interested is paramount. You have identified him. Now, *involve* him by letting him explore with a variety of media after *exposing* him to the best we have to offer, and finally, *affirm* that his creations are interesting and worthy of notice. This is the kind of guidance that will provide the stimulus and opportunities that step over the boundaries of mediocrity.

Judy Myers Bellemere
Mary Judith Bellemere Stallard
Art Teachers
Shawnee Mission School District
Shawnee Mission, KS

Working With the Drama Teacher

Other students have talents in drama. Tapping into their interests can improve their willingness to learn in various content areas. Expert Harper Lee highlights strategies for letting students learn content as they develop their interests and talents in drama. Some students thrive when they have opportunities to use their interests and talents in drama to show what it is that they have learned through projects like skits, videos, and podcasts.

◇◇

SURVIVAL SECRETS FOR DEVELOPING TALENT IN DRAMA

Harper Lee

A young person gifted in drama craves work that challenges her intellectually, creatively, and kinesthetically. You might think "This particular student is a class clown or an attention-seeker; she must be gifted in drama." It's possible that the extra energy rolling off that student comes from an innate talent for performance, so don't rule her out. But don't rule out the quiet student in the back row, either. As in other subject areas, you can't know who has an aptitude for drama until you test your students, until you give them a chance, and until you give yourself a chance to see what they are made of.

Theatre can be a wonderful thing in the classroom. Work the right play into your curriculum and you can cross-pollinate content areas, addressing a variety of needs in a highly creative way. Select a Shakespearean comedy and do a unit on poetry as you study the play. Or select a Shakespearean history and delve into the Elizabethan theatre and the historical time period covered in the play. You can also take a more contemporary approach; there are plenty of playwrights writing wonderful material for young people that covers all kinds of academic ground, including math and science.

Now a difficult, but necessary, charge: Give your students an opportunity to perform. As mentioned, students gifted in drama desire and must have a chance to be in front of an audience. Cast a simple scene, allow a student to tackle a monologue, and make an audience out of other students and teachers. Don't be afraid of this process yourself. John Doyle, a very famous and successful director who has worked with actresses like Judi Dench, insists that he never goes into rehearsals knowing all of the answers—theatre is always a journey, always a learning process. Don't fret about costumes, lights, and expensive props—they don't matter. Put all of the focus on the text you have chosen, the young actors in your class, and reading. All dramatic work of any substance is grounded in research done on characters and the world of the play; great actors are greatly curious and therefore great readers.

How do you tell a young person who is gifted in drama from one who is not? Their giftedness will be as evident as another student's giftedness in another area. You are not looking for the showiest student or the loudest student. You are looking for a student who has connected to a genuine creative impulse that is unique to him. His dramatic work and performance will be honest, genuine, and very easy, delightful even, to watch.

Never underestimate how hard a young person gifted in drama is willing to work. All people who truly love drama have an insatiable appetite for it, and they want more than anything to perform substantive material for an audience.

Harper Lee
Educational Theatre Association
Cincinnati, OH

Identifying Talent in the Arts

The special teachers in your school can be terrific resources in the identification process for the visual and performing arts. Tap into their expertise for both the screening and the identification of talent in art, music, drama, and dance.

The Jot Downs for the Visual Arts and for Music (Figures 23 and 24) provide guidance for teachers as they observe behaviors of students, looking for indicators of talent in the visual arts and music. Teachers with specialization in these areas are valuable resources to take the lead in the identification process of children who are gifted and talented in the visual and performing arts.

Visual Arts Jot Down

Date ____ / ____ / ____
　　　　Mo.　Day　Yr.

Teacher ____
Grade ____ School ____

Brief description of observed activity ____

1. As students show evidence of the following characteristics in comparison with age peers, jot their names down in the appropriate box/es.
2. When recommending students for gifted services, use this identification jot down as a reminder of student performances in the visual arts.

May be asked by others to do artwork.	Likes to comment on colors, shapes, and structure of things.	May be critical of own artwork and work of others.	Enjoys and takes pride in doing visual art well.
Draws or doodles often in school or at home.	Does outstanding original artwork.	Likes the opportunity to choose to express self through the use of many different materials.	Enjoys talking about art and collecting works of art.

Figure 23. Visual arts jot down. From *Jot Downs* by M. A. Evans & L. Whaley (n.d.), unpublished manuscript, The Center for Gifted Studies, Western Kentucky University, Bowling Green, KY. Reprinted with permission of the authors.

| Masters basic art skills quickly and easily. | Has a keen sense of humor; makes unusual connections with drawing. | Concentrates on art projects for long periods; may shut out other things going on. | Creates exceptional charts, graphs, models, or other visuals when given the opportunity. |
| Provides detailed artwork (elaboration). | Has a sensitive use of line/color/texture. | Enjoys open-ended art activities; shows frustration with art projects that are very specific. | Notices and shows appreciation for beauty and aesthetic qualities. |

Figure 23, continued

Music Jot Down

Date _____ / _____ / _____
Mo.   Day   Yr.

Teacher _____
Grade _____ School _____

Brief description of
observed activity _____

1. As students show evidence of the following musical characteristics in comparison with age peers, jot their names down in the appropriate box/es.
2. When recommending students for gifted services, use this identification jot down as a reminder of student performances in music.

Perceives fine differences in sound.	Remembers melodies and can reproduce them accurately.	Is sensitive to rhythm; may tap fingers or feet while working.	Has sustained interest in musical activities.
Expresses feelings or emotions through music.	Makes up original tunes.	May hum or sing to break the silence.	Displays interest in musical symbols and learns them easily.

Figure 24. Music jot down. From *Jot Downs* by M. A. Evans & L. Whaley (n.d.), unpublished manuscript, The Center for Gifted Studies, Western Kentucky University, Bowling Green, KY. Reprinted with permission of the authors.

Identifies rhythmic patterns as same or different.	Likes to perform musically.	Sings on pitch.	Performs musically with a high degree of technical difficulty.
Displays interest in musical instruments and various ways to produce sound.	Enjoys musical performances.	Plays or would like to play a musical instrument.	Prefers to work with music playing.

Figure 24, continued

Conclusion

Using the expertise of all teachers in your building contributes to making your school one that prides itself on each child developing her potential. A team effort is always stronger than a single person trying to accomplish the same purpose.

Survival Tips

- ○ Plan with all school personnel, including the special teachers, to build a network of professionals who are on board to develop the talents of all children who express interest and demonstrate potential in any content or talent area.

- ○ Parents need to know that all school personnel are resources for talent development for their children.

Survival Toolkit

- ○ *Biographies for Talented Readers, A Bibliography* (http://www.ualr.edu/giftedctr/slufy/Biographies_for_Children.pdf): Ann Robinson at the University of Arkansas at Little Rock has put together this bibliography of biographies suitable for gifted children. The list includes the reading levels for each book.

- ○ *Reading Lists* (http://www.hoagiesgifted.com/reading_lists.htm): The Hoagies' Gifted Education Page website provides more than one list of recommended books for advanced readers on a variety of topics.

- ○ *Integrating the Arts Into the Curriculum for Gifted Students* (http://www.nagc.org/index.aspx?id=166): This article from NAGC suggests ideas for teachers to implement the arts into their core curriculum.

- ○ Cukierkorn, J. R. (2008). *Arts education for gifted learners*. Waco, TX: Prufrock Press.

- ○ Halsted, J. W. (2009). *Some of my best friends are books: Guiding gifted readers from preschool to high school* (3rd ed.). Scottsdale, AZ: Great Potential Press.

- ○ Hauser, P., & Nelson, G. A. (1988). *Books for the gifted child* (Vol. 2). New York, NY: Bowker.

20 Opportunities Galore

An opportunity is not a real opportunity until the person who might benefit from the opportunity knows about it. Never miss the chance to tell a child about an opportunity that you think is a match for a strength he has.—Julia L. Roberts and Julia Roberts Boggess

Key Question

- What contests, competitions, summer and Saturday programs, travel, and other opportunities are available in your school and community?

Be a talent development coordinator. Let the principal, the counselor, and all staff in the office know that you would like to have copies of all announcements about contests and competitions. As you gather announcements, you can share information with individual students or with classes if you think several students' interests and talents would match the opportunities available.

Your students may have passion areas you will not know about unless you ask for that information, so be sure to solicit information from students about their interests and talents outside of school, as well as more in-depth information about those interests and talents you know about from school. Then, keep track of those passion areas. Doing so will give you optimal possibilities for matching opportunities to your students. This information about student interests also lets you get to know your students better. What an asset that is!

Contests and Competitions

Contests and competitions provide opportunities for children to share their talents and incentives for working hard to improve skills in their talent areas. Recitals and other performances encourage young people to get ready to perform for others. Such events are important steps in talent development, as a young person notches up his skills and interests as he prepares for the contest or competition. Some contests and competitions provide prizes and others result in recognition. Either way, the experience can be very motivating to young people. In fact, participating in the process is a great experience in and of itself. Usually such contests provide opportunities for students to get to know others of their age, ones who share their interests. What a win it is for all concerned when children have opportunities to perform in their interest and talent areas and to meet like-minded peers.

The product, whether it is a slogan or an aria, is the critical component of a contest or competition. Clear expectations of the product itself are essential if the product is to be high quality. How can you make that happen? You could outline expectations for every product for every student interested in the competition. Or you could provide a guide that not only helps the student in developing the product, but also encourages her to consider creativity and the content expressed.

DAP Tools can be used to prepare and instruct students on what components are important in specific products. (See Figure 17 in a previous chapter.) The presentation component of the DAP Tool identifies the essential ingredients of a podcast, an essay, an experiment, a speech, or any other product that the contest requires. Even if you do not have experience with the wide range of products that may be required in a contest, the DAP Tool for that specific product can guide the student in creating an outstanding product. DAP Tools for multiple products can be found in *Assessing Differentiated Student Products* by Roberts and Inman (2009a).

Another possibility is to link the student with someone who has experience and, hopefully, talent in the product or performance area. Feedback from another person who has expertise helps the student prepare for the content or competition. Remember that experts are usually very happy to share with young people. In fact, they often want to encourage interest in their profession or hobby, so they welcome opportunities to do so. You may want to check with the Chamber of Commerce, a local university or community college, an artists' guild, as well as with other groups in your community to identify volunteers to guide your students.

Invite students who have been in a contest to come back and share what they learned from that experience. Did they have a good time? What did they learn from the experience? Do they still have the product so they could show the others or could they describe it? Could they do a similar performance? What would they do differently the next time?

Contests and competitions are available in all content areas. Some of them focus on creative thinking and problem solving, like Odyssey of the Mind, DestiNation Imagination, and the Future Problem Solving Program. Others focus on engineering tasks like FIRST LEGO League's robotics competition. *Competitions for Talented Kids* (2005) by Karnes and Riley listed contacts for an array of contests and competitions. Search out contests for a child or group of young people who have a special interest, or encourage the student to conduct an Internet search for possibilities. Keep a record of all contests and competitions for current and future use. Make a calendar of contests and their deadlines to have for reference, and post it in a prominent place.

Talent Searches

Another source of opportunities for young people can be found through programs sponsored by regional talent search centers. These centers cover all states, with each center handling students within a particular region. They conduct talent searches for students generally in seventh grade, providing the opportunity for young people to take the ACT or the SAT, assessments intended for graduating seniors. The centers also offer programming on weekends and during the summers, as well as other advanced learning opportunities. Check out these websites for information on the different talent searches available across the country:

- *The Center for Talented Youth at Johns Hopkins University* (http://cty. jhu.edu)
- *The Talent Identification Program at Duke University* (http://www.tip. duke.edu)
- *The Center for Talent Development at Northwestern University* (http:// www.ctd.northwestern.edu)
- *The Center for Bright Kids in Denver, CO* (http://www.centerforbrightkids. org)

Many of these centers now offer programs for younger students, often through online learning programs. These distance-learning courses can be used to supplement students' talents or help them try out areas that interest them in a short summer or afterschool course. Information on applying and qualifying for these programs can be found at each of the websites listed above.

Travel and Field Trips

Travel is another engaging opportunity that promotes learning. Sometimes students can travel to a nearby city or another part of the country to enhance their learning, and other times their travel experiences may take them to another part of the world, especially in study abroad or cultural exchange programs. In a time when globalization describes the world scene, opportunities to interact with individuals from other cultures are important.

Virtual field trips are an excellent opportunity for teachers to guide small groups or individual students on an adventure. When working with small groups, it is often difficult to find the money or the time to take students on actual field trips. When taking a field trip on the computer, you can travel around the world in seconds and explore inside places you couldn't easily go. Virtual field trips are an excellent tool to educate and motivate students. The following sections provide resources for travel, virtual field trips, and other interactive experiences in key content areas.

Math

- *Geometry Center* (http://www.scienceu.com/geometry): This website allows students to explore patterns, shapes, and symmetry in an interactive format.
- *Math by Design* (http://mathbydesign.thinkport.org): This website allows students to use math skills to design different architectural projects.
- *Max's Math Adventures* (http://teacher.scholastic.com/max/index.htm): Max and his best friend Ruth love math. At this site, Max will lead your students on an exploration of math concepts including patterns, graphs, addition, and subtractions.
- *Tessellations* (http://www.uen.org/utahlink/tours/tourFames.cgi?tour_id=14875;): On this virtual field trip, students will learn about and create tessellations. The site also directs you to other high-level websites that can lead to some wonderful discussions.
- *Internet Field Trips* (http://teacher.scholastic.com/fieldtrp/math.htm): There are many different math concepts discussed on these websites. Students can explore concepts including estimation, geometry, number sense, patterns, and the history of mathematics.
- *Villainy, Inc.* (http://villainyinc.thinkport.org/default.asp): This creative site allows students to take a trip "thwarting world supremacy through

mathematics." The site explores statistics and probability, algebra, geometry, decimals, percentages, negative numbers, and more.

Science

- *NASA's Jet Propulsion Lab* (JPL; http://virtualfieldtrip.jpl.nasa.gov/smmk/top): This trip allows students to browse through the JPL Museum, Mission Control, Robot Lab, and the Sun Zone. Children can pick a character and "chat" with the museum guide as they learn.
- *The Human Heart* (http://www.fi.edu/learn/heart): This virtual field trip allows students to explore the heart's development and structure. Students can follow the blood, travel through the body system, and learn how to take care of and monitor their bodies to maintain a healthy heart.
- *Microbe Zoo* (http://commtechlab.msu.edu/sites/dlc-me/zoo): When students visit Microbe Zoo, they can learn all about "the worlds of hidden microbes." The Information Booth guides students through Dirt Land, Animal Pavilion, Water World, Space Adventure, and the Snack Bar.
- *Ocean Planet* (http://seawifs.gsfc.nasa.gov/OCEAN_PLANET/HTML/ocean_planet_overview.html): This is a trip through the Ocean Planet exhibition from the Smithsonian Institution's National Museum of Natural History. Students can travel through the different exhibits by clicking on the map.
- *The Sun* (http://www.michielb.nl/sun/kaft.htm): This multimedia presentation was created for the Dutch Annual Science Day and takes students on a trip to the sun.
- *Volcanoes* (http://satftp.soest.hawaii.edu/space/hawaii/vfts/kilauea/kilauea.vfts.html): Students will enjoy this trip to learn more about volcanoes. Students can view remote sensing images of a volcano, take ground and radar tours around Kilauea Crater, and watch a video of lava entering the ocean.

Language Arts

- *Author, Author* (http://www.field-trips.org/lit/author/index.htm): This virtual field trip is a wonderful resource for children to learn how authors do what they do. Authors on the trip include Eric Carle, Stan and Jan Berenstain, and Judy Blume.
- *My Brother's Keeper* (http://members.cox.net/banjo1959/vt.html): This trip allows students to delve further into the Civil War and visit sites from the historical novel of the same name.

Social Studies

- *Ancient Egyptian Pyramids* (http://www.pbs.org/wgbh/nova/pyramid): This virtual field trip allows students to journey through the Great Pyramid's chambers and passageways. Students follow a group of archaeologists and learn about pharaohs.
- *Europe* (http://www.virtourist.com/index.html): Students can explore their way around the European continent on this site. The photographs of each locale are beautiful, and the tours are very descriptive.
- *U.S. Capitol Tour* (http://senate.gov/vtour/index.html): This trip allows students to click on various places in the U.S. Capitol building. They will see a panoramic view of the rooms and have the opportunity to read about historical events connected to each room.
- *White House Tour* (http://www.whitehouse.gov/about/interactive-tour): Students can click on different areas of the White House to view photographs and videos of its rooms and grounds.

Art

- *Destination Modern Art* (http://www.moma.org/interactives/destination/#): This trip follows a little alien through New York's Museum of Modern Art. When students click on a piece of art, they are able to learn about the artist, interesting facts about the art, and tips to create their own pieces of art.
- *Leonardo da Vinci* (http://www.tramline.com/tours/cross/leo/_tourlaunch1.htm): Students will be able to take a journey through Leonardo da Vinci's life and art.
- *National Gallery of Art* (http://www.nga.gov/onlinetours/index.shtm): Students can take online tours through the National Gallery of Art. They can view the art through short or more in-depth tours.

Centers for Gifted Education

Another source for information on programming options to extend the learning of your students would be centers of gifted education. Most centers are located on university campuses. Contact the closest center and find out what opportunities are provided that would match the interests of your students. If you are not located close to one of these centers, call a university near you to see what they offer for children. Then encourage them to offer programs if they do not currently do so. A few of the centers that offer programming for young people in addition to the talent search centers are:

- *The Belin-Blank Center for Gifted Education at the University of Iowa* (http://www.education.uiowa.edu/belinblank): The Belin-Blank Center for Gifted Education at the University of Iowa is a full-service gifted education center offering assessment, counseling, outreach, and consultation. They direct professional development opportunities and sponsor a variety of educational opportunities for students, including summer programming, school-year programs (Challenge Saturdays), and the Belin-Blank Exceptional Student Talent Search.
- *The Center for Gifted Education at the University of Little Rock* (http://giftedctr.ualr.edu): The Center for Gifted Education at the University of Little Rock provides opportunities for parents, students, and educators. The opportunities for educators include professional development and Pre-AP and AP instruction. They also have pre-college programs and the 3-week Summer Laureate program for students in grades K–7.
- *The Center for Gifted Education at the College of William and Mary* (http://www.cfge.wm.edu): The Center for Gifted Education at The College of William and Mary is a research and development center. The center provides a variety of services and training for adults interested in learning more about working with gifted individuals. These services include an AP Institute, National Curriculum Network Conference (NCNC), and customized professional development. They offer enrichment opportunities for students, including summer opportunities and a career and academic planning experience for high-ability students.
- *The Center for the Education and Study of Gifted, Talented, Creative Learners at the University of Northern Colorado* (http://www.unco.edu/cebs/gtcenter): The center for the Education and Study of Gifted, Talented, Creative Learners at the University of Northern Colorado provides opportunities for students, parents, and educators. Student programming includes the Summer Enrichment Program. The center offers workshops and symposia for parents and educators of gifted children.
- *The Center for Gifted Studies at Western Kentucky University* (http://wku.edu/gifted): The Center for Gifted Studies offers year-round opportunities for young people who are gifted as well as for educators and parents. Professional development opportunities include an Advanced Placement Institute, workshops on social-emotional development of gifted children, leadership development, and twice-exceptional children. The center offers summer programming for middle and high school students and Super Saturdays for first through eighth graders. The center has advocacy as one major primary focus.
- *The Frances A. Karnes Center for Gifted Studies at the University of Southern Mississippi* (http://www.usm.edu/gifted): The Frances A. Karnes Center for Gifted Studies at the University of Southern

Mississippi provides a variety of opportunities for youth, parents, and educators. The programming for youth includes Saturday and summer programs as well as the Career Explorations for Girls Conference. Parent resources include the Parenting Gifted Children Conference. The programming for educators includes the Day of Sharing for Teachers of the Gifted.

Conclusion

Opportunities abound, and you may be the one, perhaps the only one, to connect young people with opportunities that match their strengths and interests. It is so important to know your students; in fact, that is a must if you are able to match students with various contests, competitions, extracurricular opportunities, virtual or actual travel and experiences, as well as summer and Saturday programs. Such opportunities can help students find interests that last a lifetime.

Survival Tips

- You may be the only one to let a young person know about a contest or competition, a Saturday or summer program, or any other opportunity that you think matches his interests, skills, and talents. Don't miss the chance to do so.

- Competitions and contests, as well as Saturday and summer programs, often are the deciding factors as to what the young person decides to major in during her college years. These opportunities are not frivolous but essential in helping students make friends who share their interests and goals, as well as for engaging students in learning in a high-interest content or talent area.

Survival Toolkit

- *Contests and Awards* (http://www.hoagiesgifted.org/contests.htm): This page of the Hoagies' Gifted Education Page website offers links to contest and scholarship opportunities for gifted students.

- *Summer and Saturday Programs* (http://www.hoagiesgifted.org/summer.htm): This page of the Hoagies' Gifted Education Page website provides links to hundreds of opportunities for gifted kids, organized by state.

○ *Summer Opportunities for Gifted Kids* (http://www.nagc.org/index. aspx?id=1103): This page of the NAGC website includes links to articles on the benefits of summer camps and programs for gifted students, along with access to the NAGC Resource Directory, which lists many such programs.

○ Berger, S. L. (2008). *The ultimate guide to summer opportunities for teens: 200 programs that prepare you for college success.* Waco, TX: Prufrock Press.

○ Karnes, F. A., & Riley, T. L. (2005). *Competitions for talented kids.* Waco, TX: Prufrock Press.

○ Roberts, J. L., & Inman, T. F. (2009). *Assessing differentiated student products: A protocol for development and evaluation.* Waco, TX: Prufrock Press.

21 Unlocking Considerations That Often Mask Giftedness

Foster a supportive ecosystem that nurtures and celebrates excellence and innovative thinking. Parents/guardians, education professionals, peers, and students themselves must work together to create a culture that expects excellence, encourages creativity, and rewards the successes of all students regardless of their race/ethnicity, gender, socioeconomic status, or geographical locale.—National Science Board (2010, p. 3)

Key Question

- What are barriers that sometimes keep gifted children from being recognized as gifted—those who underachieve, who are in kindergarten or first grade, who are twice-exceptional, who have high energy (or ADHD), or who have a language other than English as their first language?

Gifted children may have their talents masked by underachievement, a disability, a lack of opportunity, others' expectations of their abilities for their age, or having English as a second language. Many factors can disguise or cover up the gifts or strengths that some children possess, unless the child has the opportunity to demonstrate what she can do

Underachievement

When a child does not have continuous opportunities to learn new things on an ongoing basis (remember the Bill of Rights in Chapter 8), he has not learned to be resilient when he faces an academic challenge and persistent when he needs to work through a problem. He has not developed a work ethic on academic tasks, as it is not possible to really work hard when what is being required is not difficult but rather perfunctory. Think for a moment about something you are asked to do that has become very routine such as running the vacuum. There is no way for you to do a better job, no matter how many times you vacuum, assuming that you know how to vacuum.

Underachievement is pervasive in classrooms in which young people are not required to work hard on engaging tasks in order to get high grades. It is easy for a child who has not been challenged to underachieve when faced with a challenge. Underachievement is fairly common among advanced learners.

The best way to deal with underachievement is to prevent it from happening. Teachers who preassess and match the learning experiences to the preassessment data are unlikely to face underachievement problems. It is so much better to prevent underachievement than to try to reverse it, as bad habits develop when children are not challenged. For example, idle time can result in behaviors that are unwanted in a classroom—rushing through tasks to get them done or seemingly not paying attention in class, but doing the work.

Del Siegle provides a description of underachievement, with recommendations for addressing this pervasive problem.

SURVIVAL SECRETS FOR REVERSING UNDERACHIEVEMENT AMONG GIFTED STUDENTS

Del Siegle

Julia believes English is not important and seldom completes her English writing assignments. Carlos dislikes his history teacher and refuses to put any effort into history projects. Damian believes mathematics is too difficult and does not attempt any work associated with it. Each of these students is underachieving for a different reason. All students have the ability to learn and attain self-fulfillment; however, many students are at risk of failing to achieve their academic potential. The reasons often vary from student to student.

Gifted students are one group of learners who are not normally considered at risk for academic failure; however, the seeming lack of motivation of many academically gifted students is an area of frustration and concern for many parents and teachers. Underachievement is the most frequently cited concern of educators of the gifted (Renzulli, Reid, & Gubbins, 1991). Low academic motivation affects students' current performance and their persistence at completing tasks; it ultimately limits their future choices. The underachievement of gifted students is not only a resource loss for the nation, but also a personal loss of self-fulfillment for the underachieving individual.

Underachievement tends to appear in middle school and often continues into high school. Almost half of the gifted students who underachieve in seventh grade continue to underachieve throughout junior high and high school (Peterson & Colangelo, 1996), and while many attend college, only about half finish college in 4 years (Peterson, 2000). In the largest longitudinal study of underachievers conducted to date, McCall, Evahn, and Kratzer (1992) found that 13 years after high school, the educational and occupational status of high school underachievers paralleled their grades in high school, rather than their abilities. They also found that underachievers were less likely to complete college and remain in their jobs.

Generally, underachievers are more likely to be male than female. The ratio of male underachievers to female underachievers appears to be at least 2:1 (Baker, Bridger, & Evans, 1998; Matthews & McBee, 2007; McCall, 1994; McCoach, 2002; McCoach & Siegle, 2001; Peterson & Colangelo, 1996; Richert, 1991; Siegle, Reis, & McCoach, 2006).

Peer issues may influence the achievement and underachievement of adolescents. High-achieving peers can contribute to some students' reversal of their underachievement (Reis, Hébert, Diaz, Maxfield, & Ratley, 1995). Likewise, negative peer attitudes often relate to underachievement (Clasen & Clasen, 1995; Weiner, 1992). Underachieving students frequently report peer influence as the strongest force impeding their achievement, and many report peer pressure or the attitude of the other kids, including friends, as the primary force against getting good grades (Clasen & Clasen, 1995). Students with friends who care about learning

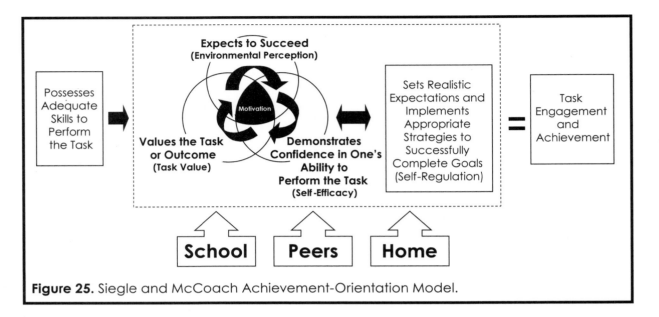

Figure 25. Siegle and McCoach Achievement-Orientation Model.

demonstrate better educational outcomes than those in less educationally oriented peer groups (Chen, 1997). When examining students' fall and spring grades, students' grades more closely resemble their friends' at the end of the school year than they do at the beginning of the school year; students' grades tend to decrease between fall and spring if their friends have lower grades in the fall. Although peer achievement levels do relate to students' academic achievement, it is unclear whether the choice to associate with other nonachievers is a cause or a result of gifted students' underachievement. Although some gifted students underachieve because they have not had opportunities to develop their potential, others choose not to develop their potential. Siegle and McCoach (2002) suggested that students who underachieve may espouse one of three problematic beliefs: (1) They do not believe they have the skills to do well (self-efficacy) and are afraid to try and fail; (2) they do not see the work they are being asked to do as meaningful (task value); or (3) they believe the "deck is stacked against them" (environmental perceptions) and any effort they put forth will be thwarted. When any one of these negative beliefs exists, students tend not to perform well (see Figure 25).

Students must believe they have the skills to perform a task before they will attempt it. For example, students must believe they are capable in mathematics before they will attempt a difficult math problem. If they believe mathematics is too difficult, they are unlikely to put forth appropriate effort. Motivated students believe they have the skills to do well in school. It is also imperative that students recognize their own role in developing these skills (Siegle, 2008). Students who believe their abilities are not innate but have been developed are more likely to attempt challenging tasks (Dweck, 2000). Gifted students are at risk for believing their abilities are simply innate, particularly if others in their lives have not discussed their giftedness with them. It is important for gifted children to recognize that the talents they possess are acquired, that they have something to do with mastering them, and that they are capable of further developing these talents and even learning new ones.

For many students, school is not meaningful. This is particularly true for many gifted students who are not being intellectually challenged in their classrooms. When students value the goals of school, they are more likely to engage in academics, expend more effort on their schoolwork, and do better academically (Pintrich & DeGroot, 1990; Wigfield, 1994). There is a positive relationship between students' interest in a subject area and their assessment of their skill in that area. Students who report being interested in an area tend to do well; those with lower interest also have lower self-reported achievement (Siegle, Rubenstein, Pollard, & Romey, 2010). Educators can make learning meaningful by helping students develop a personal value for learning by reflecting on how their lives will be different by learning, or not learning, given school content (Kaplan, 2006). Educators must also do a better job of sharing why content is pertinent (Brophy, 2008).

Students' perceptions of their environment play an important role in their achievement motivation. Students must expect to succeed and know that those around them will support their efforts. They must trust that their efforts will not be thwarted by external factors and that putting forth effort is not a waste of time and energy. Students who view their environment as friendly and reinforcing may be more likely to demonstrate motivated behavior. Phrases such as "My teacher does not like me" or "I cannot learn the way he teaches" may be signs that students do not view their environment as friendly or that they have developed a belief that their efforts do not affect outcomes. Some environmental factors are within an individual's control, others are not.

People put their effort into areas where they believe they can be successful and in environments where they believe they are supported (Ogbu, 1978).

Although each of the three attitudes discussed above is important, it is their interaction that results in engagement and performance. Motivated students feel good about their abilities, find the tasks in which they are engaged meaningful, and feel supported and appreciated in their environment. The intensity of the attitudes in the three areas need not be equally strong; however, attitudes must be positive in each area. Ultimately, the three attitudes direct a resultant behavior (self-regulation) that results in achievement. If any one of the three components is low, regardless of the strength of the others, motivation is hindered. When students value the task or outcome and have positive perceptions of themselves and their opportunities for success, they are more likely to implement self-regulation strategies that result in students setting realistic expectations and applying appropriate strategies for academic success.

Del Siegle, Ph.D.
University of Connecticut
Storrs, CT

◇◇◇

Young Gifted Children

Young gifted children constitute a special group that contains much promise that can be blunted if their schools do not offer ongoing opportunities to learn new things (because these children already have learned much of what is expected at that level). Thus, young gifted children often have their abilities masked and, consequently, they may learn to underachieve.

Patrice McCrary discusses the challenges that can be offered in an early childhood classroom, and she describes what young children can achieve when the learning ceiling is removed.

SURVIVAL SECRETS ON INFLUENCING EARLY CHILDHOOD LEARNING

Patrice McCrary

As a curriculum coordinator for an elementary school, I had the enjoyable task of assessing primary students teachers nominated for the primary talent pool. Often those students amazed me with their knowledge in certain content areas well beyond expectations for a child that age. I always eagerly asked, "Who taught you that?" The comment was always something along the lines of a parent or even a grandparent. Never did I hear the response, "My teacher." I became concerned that we were building classrooms of middle-of-the-road expectations. What could I, as a regular education teacher, do to make certain a child's response was, "My teacher taught me that!" when asked about a brilliant piece of knowledge? I requested to return to the classroom as a kindergarten teacher with a mission. Yes, the students who struggled would receive the support they needed, but those students ready to fly would soon soar.

My earlier years of teaching were filled with making certain I followed the teacher editions to cover the content. I should have been busy having the children uncover the content and following their needs. I became an avid kid watcher/assessor/facilitator. Assessments became driving forces in the classroom. If a child already knew the content, then she was ready to move beyond that level. How exciting it became to assess a child in reading in the kindergarten classroom and discover students ready to read second-, third-, even eighth-grade-level materials! Math preassessment made it easy to group children. I now love working with 5-year-olds as they determine whether or not a particular number is a prime number. The children in room 80 have never been told they will learn more about a concept later. In our classroom, later is now.

When parents tell me their child has gone beyond their own level of knowledge, my heart sings. In science, the children learn about neutral buoyancy through inquiry learning experiences. In math, they discover that a square is a rectangle, but a rectangle is not a square. In reading, they quickly share that they are reading with inflection as a visitor stops nearby to listen. A group of children gather around a globe to determine which countries are on what continents . . . just because they want to know. Every kindergarten student and every classroom can have these experiences. It simply takes a teacher willing to remove the ceiling of learning. My students soar, and I love being the flight attendant.

Patrice McCrary
Kindergarten Teacher, Cumberland Trace Elementary School
Bowling Green, KY
2003 Kentucky Teacher of the Year
2009 National Teacher Hall of Fame Inductee
National Board Certified Teacher

Gifted Students With Disabilities

A category of gifted children that is often new to educators is the gifted student who also has a disability, commonly referred to as a twice-exceptional student. For many of these students, their disabilities can mask their gifts, leaving them unidentified for advanced programs. In some cases, a student's gifts can mask her disabilities, making teachers think the student is working at a level average to her peer group. Elizabeth Nielson and Dennis Higgins make recommendations to help parents and educators understand the needs of this group of young people.

SURVIVAL SECRETS FOR UNDERSTANDING THE NEEDS OF TWICE-EXCEPTIONAL CHILDREN

Elizabeth Nielsen and Dennis Higgins

As the population of gifted students who also have disabilities or challenge areas increases, so does the challenge a classroom teacher faces in order to meet the needs of these unique, often emotional students. It is especially difficult when the needs of the twice-exceptional student behave like a moving target. Just when the teacher feels the right path has been located and success is on the horizon, the challenge seems to morph into an additional, more difficult condition. This is the reality for children whom the field of gifted education describes as twice-exceptional learners. The difficulties these children raise are neither intentional nor purposeful on the student's part. It is the honest but confusing reality these individuals present to teachers and parents.

The characteristics of a twice-exceptional child read like a Mobius strip acts: superior vocabulary, but poor social skills; advanced ideas and opinions, but high sensitivity to criticism; penetrating insight into complex issues, but difficulty with written expression. These learners are frequently underidentified, misunderstood, disconnected, mysterious, bright, alone, scared, and extremely independent. When so many discrepant, opposing characteristics appear within one individual, solutions and strategies to address this enigma are not always at the educator's or family's disposal.

There have been sharp debates and numerous articles about the most "appropriate" approach to instructing the twice-exceptional child. Should the teacher address the gifted needs first and then turn to the challenge areas? Or should the approach take the opposite focus? Should the teacher only address the giftedness and allow the gifts to overtake the challenge? Should the teacher address the challenges and hope the giftedness will take care of itself? Should the teacher focus on the emotional side of the student first and foremost? Unfortunately, in fact, these are the easier questions. The more difficult issue concerns the long-term effects of instruction on the lives of twice-exceptional children. How will the experience in the classroom of today influence the reality of the students' tomorrows? How can we prepare these children to work in situations where the environment is not accepting of their challenge? How can we help these children negotiate a life filled with exogenous factors? How can we help these students take charge of their own amazing promise?

John Dewey has emphasized the need for experiential, inquiry-based instruction, stating that experience is *of* as well as *in* nature. It is *how* the individual experiences the event that is important. Educating and raising a twice-exceptional learner is destined to be a powerfully rewarding experience for everyone involved. The process does not always guarantee a product and the conclusions are not necessarily universal. But it is a road that must be traveled.

M. Elizabeth Nielsen, Ph.D.
Associate Professor of Special Education at the University of New Mexico
Honorary Member of the Colorado Academy of Educators for the Gifted, Talented, and Creative

L. Dennis Higgins, Ed.D.
Adjunct Professor of Gifted Education at the University of New Mexico
Honorary Member of the Colorado Academy of Educators for the Gifted, Talented, and Creative

◇◇

One of the best strategies for bringing out the best in gifted children who also have a disability is to focus on their strengths while accommodating the disability. It is unproductive to focus on deficiencies alone. Temple Grandin (Peif, 2011), a professor and researcher with autism, has said that schools focus too much on socialization skills and need to spend more time on hands-on learning. She said, "I was making things all the time as a child. Things I got fixated on, I got motivated on. Teachers need to harness that fixation" (para. 15).

ADD/ADHD or High Energy

Another issue that can cloud appropriate educational opportunities for children concerns the appropriate identification of a child as having Attention Deficit/Hyperactivity Disorder (ADHD). Sometimes a child with high energy is misdiagnosed as having ADHD when the child is actually gifted and demonstrating behaviors that are characteristic of gifted children and of children with ADHD. Sharon Lind (1996) put together a chart (see Table 5) that described behaviors that are characteristic of a child who is gifted and of one who has ADHD. This chart allows parents and teachers to distinguish between behaviors typical of each label.

English Language Learners

English language learners (ELLs) constitute a category of children that includes those who are gifted and talented; however, it may be difficult to identify them as advanced learners as they are currently learning a new language. Often their ability in math reveals itself before abilities in other areas, as the language barrier hampers the child's chance to show his verbal abilities. Using

Table 5
Checklist to Consider Before Referring a Gifted Child for ADHD Evaluation

Gifted?	Need More Information	ADD/ADHD?
Contact with intellectual peers diminishes inappropriate behavior		Contact with intellectual peers has no positive effect on behavior
Appropriate academic placement diminishes inappropriate behavior		Appropriate academic placement has no positive effect on behavior
Curricular modifications diminish inappropriate behavior		Curricular modifications have no effect on behavior
The child has logical (to the child) explanations for inappropriate behavior		Child cannot explain inappropriate behavior
When active, child enjoys the movement and does not feel out of control		Child feels out of control
Learning appropriate social skills has decreased "impulsive" or inappropriate behavior		Learning appropriate social skills has not decreased "impulsive" or inappropriate behavior
Child has logical (to the child) explanations why tasks, activities are not completed		Child is unable to explain why tasks, activities are not completed
Child displays fewer inappropriate behaviors when interested in subject matter or project		Child's behaviors are not influenced by his or her interest in the activity
Child attributes excessive talking or interruptions on need to share information, need to show that he/she knows the answer, or need to solve a problem immediately		Child cannot attribute excessive talking or interruptions to a need to learn or share information
Child who seems inattentive can repeat instructions		Child who seems inattentive is unable to repeat instructions
Child thrives on working on multiple tasks—gets more done, enjoys learning more		Child moves from task to task for no apparent reason
Inappropriate behaviors are not persistent—seem to be a function of subject matter		Inappropriate behaviors persist regardless of subject matter
Inappropriate behaviors are not persistent—seem to be a function of teacher or instructional style		Inappropriate behaviors persist regardless of teacher or instructional style
Child acts out to get teacher attention		Child acts out regardless of attention

Developed by Sharon Lind. Copyright 1996 Sharon Lind. Reprinted with permission of the author.

nonverbal assessment is preferable for recognizing exceptional ability for English language learners.

Conclusion

All children should have opportunities to achieve their potentials, including those who are gifted and talented. The phrase "all children" also includes children of all ages, those from all economic levels and geographic regions, as well as those who don't appear to be gifted due to their behaviors, language, or disability. Although issues can cloud the picture for some gifted young people to achieve what their potentials would predict, you and your colleagues can educate parents and teachers in order for them to be aware of barriers and strategies to overcome the barriers. Our society cannot afford to lose talent; instead you must be in the business of talent development.

Survival Tips

- O Gifted children may have their talents masked by a disability, a lack of opportunity, a preconceived idea of what ADHD and/or high energy looks like, what a young child should be able to do, or having English as a second language.

- O Keep learning about issues that mask giftedness.

- O Parents need to know that giftedness will not always reveal itself at all, much less in the same way. Consult with professionals who are knowledgeable about gifted children about any special issues regarding your children who have been identified as gifted and talented or that you suspect should be.

Survival Toolkit

- O *2E Twice-Exceptional Newsletter* (http://www.2enewsletter.com): This newsletter offers a wide variety of resources to parents and teachers of gifted students with learning disabilities.

- O *Excerpts From* Gifted Hands: The Ben Carson Story (http://www.youtube.com/watch?v=20ew5848Z8E): This Youtube video shares excerpts from *Gifted Hands: The Ben Carson Story*. Ben Carson's mother played the significant role in getting him on the achievement track, and today he is a leading neurosurgeon at Johns Hopkins University. It's a good resource to use when discussing underachievement.

- Baum, S. M., & Owen, S. V. (2004). *To be gifted and learning disabled: Strategies for helping bright students with LD, ADHD, and more.* Mansfield Center, CT: Creative Learning Press.

- Iseman, J. S., Silverman, S. M., & Jeweler, S. (2010). *101 school success tools for students with ADHD.* Waco, TX: Prufrock Press.

- Jolly, J. L., Treffinger, D., Inman, T. F., & Smutny, J. F. (2011). *Parenting gifted children: The authoritative guide from the National Association for Gifted Children.* Waco, TX: Prufrock Press.

- Matthews, M. S. (2008). *Working with gifted English language learners.* Waco, TX: Prufrock Press.

- Roffman Shevitz, B., Stemple, M., Barnes-Robinson, L., & Jeweler, S. (2011). *101 school success tools for smart kids with learning difficulties.* Waco, TX: Prufrock Press.

- Webb, J. T., Amend, E. R., Webb, N. E., Goerss, J., Beljan, P., & Olenchak, F. R. (2005). *Misdiagnosis and dual diagnoses of gifted children and adults: ADHD, bipolar, OCD, Asperger's, depression, and other disorders.* Scottsdale, AZ: Great Potential Press.

- Weinfeld, R., Barnes-Robinson, L., Jeweler, S., & Roffman Shevitz, B. (2006). *Smart kids with learning difficulties: Overcoming obstacles and realizing potential.* Waco, TX: Prufrock Press.

Concluding Thoughts

There are such great opportunities ahead for you to challenge your gifted students, but you will need to embark on this journey one step at a time. Start at the very beginning:

- Learn about gifted education in your school, school district, and state.
- Find colleagues who share your interests in talent development.
- Participate in decision-making groups whenever possible. Volunteer for a curriculum committee or a committee to interview a prospective faculty member. It is so important to be "in the room" when decisions are made.
- Take the opportunity to participate in professional development related to gifted education and get fellow educators to do the same.
- Join your state advocacy organization—the local one too, if one is established.

Use *Teacher's Survival Guide: Gifted Education* as a ready reference as you work to make your school one that is known as a great place for all children to learn. Just remember that the phrase "all children" includes children who differ in many ways—those who learn at different paces, who have a wide array of interests, who have both abilities and disabilities, and who come from all backgrounds. In a school known for fulfilling its mission to develop talent, all children will thrive, and you will too.

References

Adams, C. M., & Pierce, R. L. (2006). *Differentiating instruction: A practical guide to tiered lessons in the elementary grades.* Waco, TX: Prufrock Press.

Anderson, L. W. (Ed.), Krathwohl, D. R. (Ed), Airasian, P. W., Cruikshank, K. A., Mayer, R. E., Pintrich, P. R., . . ., & Wittrock, M. C. (2001). *A taxonomy for learning, teaching, and assessing: A revision of Bloom's taxonomy of educational objectives* (Abridged ed.). New York, NY: Longman.

Assouline, S. G., Colangelo, N., Lupkowski-Shoplik, A., Forstadt, L., & Lipscomb, J. (2009). *Iowa acceleration scale* (3rd ed.). Scottsdale, AZ: Great Potential Press.

Baker, J. A., Bridger, R., & Evans, K. (1998). Models of underachievement among gifted preadolescents: The role of personal, family, and school factors. *Gifted Child Quarterly, 42,* 5–14.

Bloom, B. S. (1985). Generalizations about talent development. In B. S. Bloom (Ed.), *Developing talent in young people.* New York, NY: Ballantine.

Bridgeland, J. M. (2007). *Achievementrap announcement.* Retrieved from http://www.jkcf.org/news-knowledge/press-releases/achievement-trap-announcement

Brophy, J. (2008). Developing students' appreciation for what is taught in school. *Educational Psychologist, 43,* 132–141.

Carroll, L. (2000). *Alice's adventures in wonderland.* New York, NY: Signet Classic/New American Library. (Original work published in 1865)

Chen, X. (1997, June). *Students' peer groups in high school: The pattern and relationship to educational outcomes* (NCES 97-055). Washington, DC: U.S. Department of Education.

Clasen, D. R., & Clasen, R. E. (1995). Underachievement of highly able students and the peer society. *Gifted and Talented International, 10*(2), 67–75.

Colangelo, N., Assouline, S. G., & Gross, M. U. M. (2004). *A nation deceived: How schools hold back America's brightest students.* Iowa City: University of Iowa, The Connie Belin & Jacqueline N. Blank International Center for Gifted Education and Talent Development.

Cote, D. (2005). *Wicked: The Grimmerie: A behind-the-scenes look at the hit Broadway musical.* New York, NY: Hyperion.

Cross, T. L. (2011). *On the social and emotional lives of gifted children* (4th ed.). Waco, TX: Prufrock Press.

de Wet, C. F., Gubbins, E. J., & Vahindi, S. (Eds.). (2005). *The NRC/GT instrument bank* [CD]. Storrs: University of Connecticut, National Research Center on the Gifted and Talented.

Dweck, C. S. (2000). *Self-theories: Their role in motivation, personality, and development.* Philadelphia, PA: Psychology Press.

Dweck, C. S. (2006). *Mindset: The new psychology of success.* New York, NY: Random House.

Evans, M. A., & Whaley, L. (n.d.). *Jot downs.* Unpublished manuscript, The Center for Gifted Studies, Western Kentucky University, Bowling Green, KY.

Frasier, M. M. (1995). *A new window for looking at gifted children.* Storrs: University of Connecticut, National Research Center on the Gifted and Talented.

Friedman, T. (2009, June 27). Invent, invent, invent. *The New York Times.* Retrieved from http://www.nytimes.com/2009/06/28/opinion/28friedman.html

Friedman, T. (2010, February 23). U.S.G. and P.T.A. *The New York Times.* Retrieved from http://www.nytimes.com/2010/11/24/opinion/24friedman.html?_r=1

Gardner, H. W. (1993, July). Educating for understanding. *The American School Board Journal, 180*(7), 20–24.

Gewertz, C. (2010, August 18). ACT scores deliver good and bad news. *Education Week.* Retrieved from http://blogs.edweek.org/edweek/curriculum /2010/08/act_scores.html

Gladwell, M. (2008). *The outliers: The story of success.* New York, NY: Little, Brown.

Gordon, W. J. J. (1961). *Synectics.* New York, NY: Harper & Row.

Hébert, T. P. (2011). *Understanding the social and emotional lives of gifted students.* Waco, TX: Prufrock Press.

Higher Education Opportunity Act, Pub. L. No. 110-315 § 122 Stat. 3078 (2008).

Johnsen, S. K. (Ed.). (2011). *Identifying gifted students: A practical guide* (2nd ed.). Waco, TX: Prufrock Press.

Kanevsky, L. S. (2003). Tiering with Venn diagrams. *Gifted Education Communicator, 34*(2), 42–44.

Kaplan, S. (2006, July). Gifted students in a contemporary society: Implications for curriculum. Keynote at the 29th Annual University of Connecticut Confratute, Storrs, CT.

Karnes, F. A., & Riley, T. L. (2005). *Competitions for talented kids.* Waco, TX: Prufrock Press.

Kingore, B. (2004). *Differentiation: Simplified, realistic, and effective.* Austin, TX: Professional Associates Publishing.

Kingsolver, B. (2002, Winter). Congratulatory letter. *The Challenge, 8,* 9. Retrieved from http://www.wku.edu/Dept/Support/AcadAffairs/Gifted/giftedsite/wordpress/wp-content/uploads/2010/07/811.pdf

Kulik, J. A. (1992). *An analysis of research on ability grouping: Historical and contemporary perspectives.* Storrs: University of Connecticut, National Research Center on the Gifted and Talented.

Kulik, J. A., & Kulik, C.-L. C. (1991). Ability grouping and gifted students. In N. Colangelo & G. A. Davis (Eds.), *Handbook of gifted education* (pp. 178–196). Boston, MA: Allyn & Bacon.

Lind, S. (1996). *Before referring a gifted child for ADD/ADHD.* Retrieved from http://www.sengifted.org/articles_counseling/Lind_BeforeReferringAGiftedChildForADD.shtml

Loveless, T., Farkas, S., & Duffett, A. (2008). *High-achieving students in the era of NCLB.* Washington, DC: Thomas B. Fordham Institute.

MacGregor, M. (2010). *Everyday leadership skills and attitude inventory.* Minneapolis, MN: Free Spirit.

Marland, S. P., Jr. (1972). *Education of the gifted and talented: Report to the Congress of the United States by the U.S. Commissioner of Education and background papers submitted to the U.S. Office of Education,* 2 vols. Washington, DC: U.S. Government Printing Office. (Government Documents, Y4.L 11/2: G36)

Matthews, M. S., & McBee, M. T. (2007). School factors and the underachievement of gifted students in a talent search summer program. *Gifted Child Quarterly, 51,* 167–181.

McCall, R. B. (1994). Academic underachievers. *Current Directions in Psychological Science, 3,* 15–19.

McCall, R. B., Evahn, C., & Kratzer, L. (1992). *High school underachievers: What do they achieve as adults?* Newbury Park, CA: SAGE Publications.

McCoach, D. B. (2002). A validity study of the School Attitude Assessment Survey (SAAS). *Measurement and Evaluation in Counseling and Development, 35,* 66–77.

McCoach, D. B., & Siegle, D. (2001). A comparison of high achievers' and low achievers' attitudes, perceptions, and motivations. *Academic Exchange Quarterly, 5*(2), 71–76.

National Association for Gifted Children. (2010a). *NAGC pre-k–grade 12 gifted programming standards: A blueprint for quality gifted education programs.* Washington, DC: Author.

National Association for Gifted Children. (2010b). *Redefining giftedness for a new century: Shifting the paradigm.* Retrieved from http://www.nagc.org/index.aspx?id=6404&terms=Redefining+Giftedness

National Science Board. (2010). *Preparing the next generation of STEM innovators: Identifying and developing our nation's human capital.* Arlington, VA: National Science Foundation.

No Child Left Behind Act, 20 U.S.C. §6301 (2001).

No Child Left Behind Act, P.L. 107-110 (Title IX, Part A, Definition 22) (2002).

Ogbu, J. U. (1978). *Minority education and caste.* New York, NY: Academic Press.

Pattou, E. (2001). *Mrs. Spitzer's garden.* Orlando, FL: Harcourt.

Peif, S. (2011, February 7). Temple Grandin: Hands-on learning is key to education. *Greeley Tribune.* Retrieved from http://www.greeleytribune.com/article/200110207/NEWS/702079978

Peterson, J. S. (2000). A follow-up study of one group of achievers and underachievers four years after high school graduation. *Roeper Review, 22*, 217–225.

Peterson, J. S., & Colangelo, N. (1996). Gifted achievers and underachievers: A comparison of patterns found in school files. *Journal of Counseling and Development, 74*, 399–406.

Pintrich, P. R., & DeGroot, E. V. (1990). Motivational and self-regulated learning components of classroom academic performance. *Journal of Educational Psychology, 82*, 33–40.

Plucker, J. A., Burroughs, N., & Song, R. (2010). *Mind the (other) gap! The growing excellence gap in K–12 education.* Retrieved from http://ceep.indiana.edu/mindthegap

Reis, S. M., Hébert, T. P., Diaz, E. P., Maxfield, L. R., & Ratley, M. E. (1995). *Case studies of talented students who achieve and underachieve in an urban high school* (RM 95120). Storrs: University of Connecticut, National Research Center for the Gifted and Talented.

Reis, S. M., & McCoach, D. B. (2000). The underachievement of gifted students: What do we know and where do we go? *Gifted Child Quarterly, 44*, 152–170.

Reis, S. M., & Renzulli, J. S. (2009). Myth 1: The gifted and talented constitute one single homogeneous group and giftedness is a way of being that stays in the person over time and experience. *Gifted Child Quarterly, 53*, 233–235.

Reis, S. M., Westberg, K. L., Kulikowich, J., Caillard, F., Hebert, T. P., Plucker, J., . . ., & Smist, J. M. (1993). *Why not let high ability students start school in January? The curriculum compacting study* (Research Monograph 93106).

Storrs: University of Connecticut, National Research Center for the Gifted and Talented.

Renzulli, J. S., Heilbronner, N. N., & Siegle, D. (2010). *Think data: Getting kids involved in hands-on investigations with data-gathering instruments.* Mansfield Center, CT: Creative Learning Press.

Renzulli, J. S., Reid, B. D., & Gubbins, E. J. (1991). *Setting an agenda: Research priorities for the gifted and talented through the year 2000.* Storrs: University of Connecticut, National Research Center for the Gifted and Talented.

Renzulli, J. S., & Reis, S. M. (1997). *The Schoolwide Enrichment Model: A how-to guide for educational excellence* (2nd ed.). Mansfield Center, CT: Creative Learning Press.

Richert, E. S. (1991). Patterns of underachievement among gifted students. In J. H. Borland (Series Ed.) & M. Bireley & J. Genshaft (Vol. Eds.), *Understanding the gifted adolescent* (pp. 139–162). New York, NY: Teacher College Press.

Roberts, J. L. (n.d.). PLAN model. Unpublished manuscript, The Center for Gifted Studies, Western Kentucky University, Bowling Green, KY.

Roberts, J. L. (2006). Planning for advocacy. In J. H. Purcell & R. D. Eckert (Eds.), *Designing services and programs for high-ability learners: A guidebook for gifted education* (pp. 239–248). Thousand Oaks, CA: Corwin Press.

Roberts, J. L. (2010, Winter). Preassessment: The linchpin for defensible differentiation. *The Challenge, 24,* 10, 12.

Roberts, J. L., & Inman, T. F. (2009a). *Assessing differentiated student products: A protocol for development and evaluation.* Waco, TX: Prufrock Press.

Roberts, J. L., & Inman, T. F. (2009b). *Strategies for differentiating instruction: Best practices for the classroom* (2nd ed.). Waco, TX: Prufrock Press.

Roberts, J. L., & Inman, T. F. (2010, December). A checklist to guide advocacy for a gold standard school. *Parenting for High Potential,* 21–23.

Rogers, K. B. (2007). Lessons learned about educating the gifted and talented: A synthesis of the research on educational practice. *Gifted Child Quarterly, 51,* 382–396.

Scheve, T. (September 9, 2010). How can you tell if your child is a prodigy? Retrieved from http://health.howstuffworks.com/pregnancy-and-parenting/parenting/child-prodigy.htm

Siegle, D. (2008). The time is now to stand up for gifted education: 2007 NAGC Presidential Address. *Gifted Child Quarterly, 52,* 111–113.

Siegle, D., & McCoach, D. B. (2002). Promoting a positive achievement attitude with gifted and talented students. In M. Neihart, S. M. Reis, N. M. Robinson, & S. Moon (Eds.), *The social and emotional development of gifted children: What do we know?* (pp. 237–249). Waco, TX: Prufrock Press.

Siegle, D., Reis, S. M., & McCoach, D. B. (2006, June). *A study to increase academic achievement among gifted underachievers.* Poster presented at the 2006 Institute of Education Sciences Research Conference, Washington, DC.

Siegle, D., Rubenstein, L. D., Pollard, E., & Romey, E. (2010). Exploring the relationship of college freshman honors students' effort and ability attribution, interest, and implicit theory of intelligence with perceived ability. *Gifted Child Quarterly, 54,* 92–101.

Slavin, R. E. (1987). Ability grouping and student achievement in elementary schools: A best-evidence synthesis. *Review of Educational Research, 57,* 293–336.

Slavin, R. E. (1990). Achievement effects of ability grouping in secondary schools: A best-evidence synthesis. *Review of Educational Research, 60,* 471–499.

Slocumb, D. P. (2000). *Removing the mask: Giftedness in poverty.* Highlands, TX: aha! Process.

Southern, W. T., & Jones, E. D. (2004). Types of acceleration: Dimensions and issues. In N. Colangelo, S. G. Assouline, & M. U. M. Gross (Eds.). *A nation deceived: How schools hold back America's brightest students* (Vol. II, pp. 5–12). Iowa City: University of Iowa, The Connie Belin & Jacqueline N. Blank International Center for Gifted Education and Talent Development.

Stanley, J. C. (2000). Helping students learn only what they don't already know. *Psychology, Public Policy, and Law, 6,* 216–222.

Sternberg, R. (2000). Patterns of giftedness: A triarchic analysis. *Roeper Review, 22*(4), 231.

Subotnik, R., & Jarvin, L. (2005). Beyond expertise: Conceptions of giftedness as great performance. In R. J. Sternberg & J. E. Davidson (Eds.), *Conceptions of giftedness* (pp. 343–357). New York, NY: Cambridge University Press.

Tannenbaum, A. J. (1962). *Adolescent attitudes toward academic brilliance.* New York, NY: Teachers College Press.

Title V, Part D. [Jacob K. Javits Gifted and Talented Students Education Act of 1988], Elementary and Secondary Education Act of 1988 (2002), 20 U.S.C. sec. 7253 et seq.

Tomlinson, C. A. (2005). Traveling the road to differentiation in staff development. *JSD, The Journal of the National Staff Development Council, 26*(4), 8–12.

Treffinger, D. J. (2009). Myth 5: Creativity is too difficult to measure. *Gifted Child Quarterly, 53,* 245–247.

U.S. Department of Education. (1993). *National excellence: A case for developing America's talent.* Washington, DC: Author.

Weiner, I. B. (1992). *Psychological disturbance in adolescence* (2nd ed.). New York, NY: Wiley.

Wigfield, A. (1994). The role of children's achievement values in the self-regulation of their learning outcomes. In D. H. Schunk & B. J. Zimmerman (Eds.), *Self-regulation of learning and performance: Issues and educational applications* (pp. 101–124). Mahwah, NJ: Erlbaum.

Wyner, J. W., Bridgeland, J. M., & DiIulio, J. J. (2007). *Achievementrap: How America is failing millions of high-achieving students from lower-income families.* Lansdowne, VA: Jack Kent Cooke Foundation.

About the Authors

Julia Link Roberts, Ed.D., is the Mahurin Professor of Gifted Studies at Western Kentucky University. She is the Executive Director of The Center for Gifted Studies and the Carol Martin Gatton Academy of Mathematics and Science in Kentucky. Dr. Roberts is a member of the Executive Committee of the World Council for Gifted and Talented Children and a board member of The Association for the Gifted (a division of the Council for Exceptional Children) and the Kentucky Association for Gifted Education. Dr. Roberts received the first David W. Belin NAGC Award for Advocacy. She is coauthor with Tracy Inman of *Strategies for Differentiating Instruction: Best Practices for the Classroom* (2009 Legacy Award winner for the outstanding book for educators in gifted education by the Texas Association for the Gifted and Talented) and *Assessing Differentiated Student Products: A Protocol for Development and Evaluation*. Dr. Roberts directs summer and Saturday programs for children and young people who are gifted and talented. Dr. Roberts and her husband Richard live in Bowling Green, KY. They have two daughters, Stacy and Julia, and four grand-daughters, Elizabeth, Caroline, Jane Ann, and Claire.

Julia Roberts Boggess is an elementary librarian at Pearre Creek Elementary School in Williamson County, TN. She has taught in the primary grades and has been a gifted resource teacher. In 2008, Mrs. Boggess was awarded an $8,000 Jenny's Heroes grant from the Jenny Jones Foundation. She has taught drama and literature to elementary and middle school students in Saturday and summer programs offered by The Center for Gifted Studies at Western Kentucky University. Mrs. Boggess earned a bachelor's degree in elementary education, a master's degree in elementary education with an endorsement in gifted education, and a master's degree in library media education at Western Kentucky University. She lives in Tennessee with her husband, Mark, and her delightful daughter, Claire.